Mary's HOUSEHOLD TIPS & TRICKS

Your guide to **happiness in the home**

MARY BERRY
& LUCY YOUNG

MICHAEL JOSEPH
an imprint of
PENGUIN BOOKS

CONTENTS

―――――

―――――

'What follows are my tips for the home, gleaned from years of practical experience. I hope this will be a helping hand.'

INTRODUCTION

I've had a lot of time to gather tips and hints about cooking and how to run a house. When I was nineteen, I took a two-year course in Institutional Management at Bath College of Domestic Science. The focus was on catering, but they also taught us house-wifery, as it was referred to then. Our principal, Miss Neilson, used to sit us down and teach us the basics: laying the table, making beds and cleaning loos, among other things. They might all sound like common sense but I am very grateful to her for the knowledge she shared!

My mother was very frugal, something that was especially important living through the war, and I learnt a lot from her. Even with rationing, we would have pudding on Saturdays – this was only because my mother had said, 'No puddings unless you give up sugar in your tea.' My focus may have been on cooking, but it has always been centred on the home. In my books and TV programmes I am always very keen on sharing tips for preparing ahead or just making a recipe easier – I've lost count of the number of times I've written or spoken about warming lemons to make them

easier to juice! This book is a natural follow-on, though it isn't just made up of my mother's tips, or mine. It's a collection of what I've learnt over the years along with all the helpful hints that friends and family have imparted to us. People are always only too pleased to pass on a little tip – 'Did you know that a cut onion absorbs the smell of fresh paint,' they might say – and I am always only too delighted to benefit from their wisdom.

This book is about helping you with life and guiding you through chores – not about creating more work, or telling you what you should do. Some of the tips may not mean anything to you, because everybody's needs are different, but anything I suggest is included on the basis that it might make life easier.

Life isn't all about stress, and if you're in a panic, sit down with a pencil and some paper and think about how you can sort it out. I find writing things down a tremendous help. Every night I create a list of things to think about the next day, because then I can get up and know what I'm doing straight away. I've learnt this from the number of times I haven't looked at my diary first thing on a Monday morning, then suddenly remembered there's somewhere I should have been . . .

What follows are my tips for the home, gleaned from years of practical experience. I hope this will be a helping hand.

KITCHEN KNOW-HOW

The heart of the home

'A kitchen should always be practical and efficient to use, and organizing fridges, freezers and cupboards wisely will make your life easier in the long run.'

In our house, the kitchen is where everyone tends to congregate: friends, family and our two dogs. There's always something going on, or someone popping their head through the door. It is the warm centre of our home – quite literally warm, thanks to the Aga! – and the place where all decisions are made.

Over the years, I have planned several kitchens from scratch, so I've got to know what works for me. In my opinion, the kitchen should be one of the nicest rooms in the house. Most people tend not to spend much waking time in their bedrooms, whereas with a large kitchen or open-plan living room and kitchen, you're in there from the moment you get up until you go to bed, and it's most likely the area where your guests will spend time too. So it makes sense that it should be a very special room.

A kitchen should always be practical and efficient to use, and organizing fridges, freezers and cupboards wisely will make your life easier in the long run. Mealtimes don't have to be grand or complicated – people just love good home-cooked food – and washing and cleaning needn't be such a horrible chore if you stay on top of things.

STORING FOOD: FREEZERS

When I was first married, we didn't have freezers and for a long time they were a luxury item, but they are part of our lives now. People always think, 'But can I freeze it?' Well, you can freeze anything – the process stops food deteriorating, after all. That said, some things are more suitable for freezing than others because the process can affect the texture of the food. Some things really don't take kindly to freezing – smoked and fatty foods (e.g. egg-based sauces such as mayonnaise, and things containing gelatine, yoghurt and low-fat cream) are examples.

When thinking about freezing, I always say: remember that what you put in is what you are going to get out. Freezing food doesn't improve it. That means that if you put a curdled sauce or a not very well-flavoured tatty pie into your freezer, well, you're going to defrost that same curdled sauce or not very well-flavoured pie.

The freezer can be a tremendous help for busy days, or times when you know you won't want to be tied to the kitchen. The key to making the most of your freezer's potential is to remember that it's not just a place to put things that need using up, and to really think about when you might want to have some-thing prepared (or partially prepared) up your sleeve. It's all about making your life easier.

I find it useful to store spares of the sort of essentials I might very well run out of in my freezer:

- **I find semi-skimmed milk freezes best – keep a litre in the freezer so you can have tea or coffee when you come back from holiday, or have surprise visitors and have run out.**

- **Frozen peas or petit pois always cheer up a soup that looks bland or in need of some fresh veg.**

- **A loaf or even half a loaf of bread, well wrapped up, can save the day.**

- **Leftover gravy is so useful when you're doing chops or sausages as you can just reheat it. I'm married to a man who loves gravy, so I know!**

Freezers should operate at −18°C or below and actually work more efficiently when they are full, as there is less space for warm air to circulate when you open the door. So get cooking!

THINGS NOT TO FREEZE

Whether or not you can freeze something depends on how you would like to eat it when it is defrosted. It is handy to freeze a soft herb like coriander, for instance, if you have a large bunch that you are not going to use before it is past its best. However, frozen coriander is best added to something cooked, like a curry, as its texture when defrosted won't be the same as fresh coriander. Here are some things that don't freeze well – and any exceptions to bear in mind.

When it comes to packaged foods, always follow the instructions on the label.

Whole eggs: These are not suitable for freezing raw and in their shell, as the contents can expand and explode. Boiled eggs don't fare well either, as the white becomes rubbery.

Raw eggs can be frozen if beaten together, and separated whites can be frozen too (see page 20).

Vegetables, salad leaves and herbs that you intend to eat raw: The high water content of green leaves such as lettuce, watercress, rocket, and fruit and veg like radishes, mushrooms, cucumber, celery and tomatoes, means that they are not suitable for freezing.

Cooked spinach leaves, chopped tomatoes and chopped herbs are suitable for freezing if you plan to cook them – by adding them to a sauce, for example.

Mashed potato: Mash does not freeze very well – with shepherd's pie, for example, I prefer to freeze the meat base on its own, and add the fresh mash before putting it into the oven.

Cooked meat: Large cooked meat joints don't freeze well.

Fish roe and fish that you intend to eat raw: Sashimi grade fish should be eaten only when very fresh.

Smoked salmon can be frozen (follow the package instructions, but it's usually advisable to freeze on the day of purchase and for no longer than 3 months).

Pasta: Cooked pasta does not freeze well, unless it's in dishes like lasagne or tortellini.

Fried foods: Generally, the crisp texture of fried foods does not survive the freezing process.

Breadcrumbs do freeze well and are handy to have for when you want to do some frying. Croutons are the exception to the rule and can be fried and frozen.

Full-fat milk, single cream, sour cream, custard and yoghurt: All of these tend to separate and become watery.

Cream that has been incorporated into sauces can be frozen.

Cake icing: I prefer to freeze cakes without any icing, and ice them once they come out of the freezer. Fresh icing looks better too.

Emulsified sauces, such as mayonnaise and hollandaise: These sauces separate on defrosting.

Whole blocks of low-fat cheese, soft cheese and cottage cheese: These do not retain their texture.

Grated hard cheese freezes very well and is handy for sprinkling over dishes before cooking.

Unripe bananas: These aren't going to ripen in the freezer!

Ripe bananas can be peeled and sliced, then frozen – they are very useful for throwing into smoothies.

SEPTEMBER

11 MONDAY

12 TUESDAY   • Really Good
Beef Stew —
for 4 people

13 WEDNESDAY

14 THURSDAY

PACKAGING, LABELLING
& SCHEDULING

The aim when you put something into the freezer is to keep out air, so if you're putting something into a polythene bag, push out any air before sealing it. If you are freezing something with a sticky topping, pop it into the freezer – uncovered – for a few hours or until it's frozen solid, then carefully pack it, expelling any air.

Proper labelling is the efficient freezer's best friend. You may think you'll know what's in that funny packet with no label, but you won't. Beware the surprise meal: I've been to a friend's and we've cut into a pie that was meant to be steak, only to find that it was rhubarb! So labelling really is all-important.

Think about how you eat and what you enjoy – if you love Bolognese and eat it once every week or so, then you may as well cook a kilo of mince instead of 500g and freeze little containers for other nights when you might not get home so early. It may seem an obvious point, but don't put things in the freezer that you don't really like – otherwise, you can be sure that they will still be there in a year.

Be specific when you're labelling – say you're cooking supper and have made double quantities of stew: when you're packing up the leftovers don't just write 'Beef stew' on the bag. Think about when you're going to eat it before storing it in the freezer. Be realistic and look in your diary and write, 'Really good beef stew for 4 for 12 September', or 'Good stew, add more stock to serve'.

When you're thinking about packaging for the freezer, **choose a container and fill it up**: if you half fill it you're taking up more space than you need. If you have a pint of stock, put it in a pint container.

If you're making a bulk batch of soup, pour it into a container that is the **same size as the portion** you will serve when you come to use it. When I'm storing my soup, I tend to do a pint for two; if you're always four, put it in a two-pint container.

Ideally, use containers that stack on top of each other and **fit neatly into your freezer**: these are sold everywhere now. The thrifty freezer owner might save old plastic ice cream containers: many brands come in handy 1.5 litre sizes and if it's something you are fond of, you may end up with a few that stack nicely on top of each other!

In general, **containers are much more useful than bags,** which tend to freeze into funny shapes, making it difficult to store them neatly. However, if you haven't got a lot of plastic containers (and they do tend to disappear) you can work around this by lining a container with a plastic freezer bag, then pouring the liquid or ladling the food in carefully. When it's absolutely cold, put it into the freezer until it's frozen in a block shape; remove the block-shaped bag and you have your container back again.

Foil containers with paper lids are great for freezing crumbles (or the fruit base for a crumble), because once it's defrosted, you can pop the whole thing in the oven to cook – without its paper lid, of course. Be careful handling these foil containers, though, as they do vary in quality and strength: you might like to place them on a baking tray in order to take them in and out of the oven more easily.

HOW LONG CAN YOU FREEZE SOMETHING FOR?

- Always follow the instructions on the back of packaged foods.

- Some things freeze exceedingly well: generally, the bigger the piece of **raw meat**, the better it freezes. Freezing a piece of **cooked meat** is a different thing, though. I'd only advise doing it for a short period of time. If you've got half a leg of lamb left over from Sunday lunch, say, you can freeze it for another occasion: put a note in your diary. Use it within a fortnight, and don't forget to freeze the gravy as well. That'll be a weekday supper you don't have to think about, which is very useful.

- Unless you know exactly when the **fish** you bought was caught, freezing it is not to be recommended – often it has travelled a great distance, and may have already been frozen. If fish has been previously frozen this does not necessarily mean it is unsuitable for freezing, but it should be frozen immediately after purchase and consumed by its use-by date or within one month. Ask your fishmonger or, if buying from a supermarket, read the information on the label carefully.

- **Bread and cakes** (without icing) can be frozen for up to 2 months.

- **Milk** can be frozen, but semi-skimmed and skimmed fare better than whole milk, because of their lower fat content. Useful for when you get back from holiday and want a cup of coffee or tea without having to go to the shops! Milk can be frozen for up to a month – the same goes for homemade ice cream, which doesn't contain the same stabilizers as shop-bought.

- **Soups and stews** can be frozen for up to 3 months.

- **Stock** can be frozen for up to 2 months.

- **Leftover egg whites** can be frozen in an airtight container for up to 6 months. There's no danger in freezing them for longer, the flavour just won't be quite as good.

Freezing does not kill bacteria, so always exercise caution – if you take something out of the freezer and you're not sure about it (maybe you forgot to label it and can't be certain how long it's been in there), it probably isn't worth the risk.

FREEZER TIPS

USING UP ODDS & ENDS

When opening your freezer and looking for inspiration, it's very tempting to just reach for the big thing that's beautifully fresh, and not investigate any further. When you reach the stage when you simply have to sort out your freezer (for me, this tends to be when the door won't shut), you might stumble across a couple of sausages and think that they would have done very nicely in the pasta sauce you made last week, had you only remembered they were there . . .

A girlfriend gave me an excellent tip to avoid this: put all the little odd bits that you have knocking around – stray sausages, portions of shepherd's pie, small containers of stewed fruit – into one box or basket. This way, they will be the first thing that you glance at before you take anything else out of the freezer, and you won't miss an opportunity to make the most of them.

To be extra organized, try to freeze similar foods together, e.g. meat and fish on one shelf; fruit, veg, pastry and desserts on another. The top shelf should always be the home for odd bits and bobs: breadcrumbs, ice cubes, herbs.

FREEZING LIQUIDS

I always try to freeze liquids – like stock – in quarter, half or one pints. Many recipes say, 'add half a pint', so if you freeze it in these quantities you can just take it out and it's already measured for you.

When you've made a very good gravy for a roast, but still have half a pint left, it's so useful to put that into the freezer (label it, 'really good lamb gravy'). My husband likes gravy with his grilled chops, so next time you have grilled chops – or whatever you like to have gravy with – you just take it out, thaw it and serve it.

Stews freeze wonderfully and are brilliant to have tucked away for days when you don't have time to cook. But think about what you're eating too. An ingredient like mushrooms may not freeze particularly well – they can go a little soggy when thawed, because of their water content. So think ahead: turn fresh mushrooms (whole if small, sliced if larger) in a bit of butter, season, and toss them into the defrosted stew before reheating. This will lift the whole thing and make it taste freshly done. The same is true of carrots, celery and other vegetables. Adding fresh herbs also makes all the difference.

DEFROSTING FOOD

I generally always defrost overnight in the fridge, and wouldn't ever recommend cooking from frozen – unless you are cooking chips. You can defrost liquids in a microwave before reheating, but on the whole it's always better to defrost slowly and safely.

- **Always ensure that food that has been defrosted is piping hot throughout before serving.**

- **Eat meat within 24 hours of defrosting.**

The great exception is, of course, something large like a turkey, simply because it's not practical to store it in the fridge. At Christmas you are probably using your fridge for everything else, so there's no space for defrosting the turkey – or indeed a large gammon. Instead, put it in a cold garage (in a box, where no one can get at it) or in a cupboard in the kitchen (on a tray) – and remember that you've got it there. And bear in mind that, if the weather's cold, it will take a long time to fully defrost – up to 3 days – so plan ahead.

DEFROSTING YOUR FREEZER

There's no time limit or rule to how often you should defrost your freezer. Really, it depends how often you open the freezer door – every time you do so, ice crystals form – and whether it's in a warm place or a colder place.

Choose a day when you're not busy, then take everything out of the freezer and put it in a pile together in a cool corner – you could fill your kitchen sink or the bath with it – then cover it with tea towels and a duvet or an old sleeping bag, just something to insulate it.

Turn the freezer off at the mains, and put an old towel at the bottom of it (or you could use a roasting tin) to absorb any drips.

③

Fill a big saucepan of water – make sure it's not so heavy when filled that you can't carry it, and also that it fits into your freezer – then cover with a lid and bring to the boil on your cooker. If you don't have a saucepan that will fit into your freezer, boil the kettle and fill heatproof containers or roasting dishes with hot water instead.

④

Place a tea towel on a shelf and put the saucepan on top of it, then take the lid off. The lid will be very hot, so put it on another shelf, then shut the freezer door. The steam will melt the ice. It might seem tempting, but never try to scrape at the ice with a sharp implement! You risk piercing the freezer lining and also injuring yourself.

⑤

When the saucepan of water cools down, return it to the cooker, boil it up again and repeat until your freezer has fully defrosted. Take out the shelves and wash them with hot water and washing-up liquid, and wipe the inside of the freezer out thoroughly.

⑥

While the freezer is defrosting, have a jolly good look at all the things you've taken out of it before you put them back in again. Think, 'Am I going to keep some of those out for tonight?' and 'Are these really things I'm going to use?'

⑦

Sort everything into groups – it's always a good idea to put meat and fish, fruit, and baked goods on three separate shelves. Relabel anything that's not immediately clear. Make the most of the time while you're waiting for the ice to melt and use it to try to get yourself a bit organized: make a list of everything you've taken out and are putting back in, so that you know what's in the freezer without having to rifle through it. Then, next time you're in the kitchen, listening to the radio or watching the telly, you can look at that list and say, 'Ah, I'll use that up for supper tomorrow night,' or 'Gosh, I forgot I had that.' You can pin the list on the fridge or a wall if you like, so that you look at it every time you go to get something out. Strike off things as you use them, and try to remember to jot down new things that you put in.

⑧

Half an hour before returning everything you are keeping to the freezer, switch it back on again. You will feel so bloomin' virtuous once you've done it and you'll wonder why you didn't do it earlier.

FRIDGES

If your kitchen is on the smaller side, a tall fridge that takes up less floor area is a more sensible use of space than a wider one. What kind of storage you have in your fridge will depend on the make.

I'm very methodical when it comes to the rest of the kitchen, but the fridge is another story, so it's a case of do as I say, not do as I do . . . but here are some general pointers.

STORING FOOD

- Perishable foods should be stored between 0°C and 5°C (and always below 5°C). Brands differ, but most fridges typically have a dial to adjust the setting – check the instruction manual!

- Cool down leftovers as quickly as possible (they can be left to cool at room temperature for up to 2 hours) and eat within 2 days. Don't place still-hot food in the fridge as it will raise the temperature, which is harmful for the other food in there.

- Wrap things properly: if you don't, they will dry out.

- The coldest part of your fridge is at the bottom – and in the actual fridge itself, not in the door – which is why you should always store poultry there.

- As with cooked food that has been defrosted, it is incredibly important to ensure that any cooked chilled food is piping hot throughout when you are reheating it.

ORGANIZATION

- Isolate smelly things: it's a good idea to have a clip-lock container for all your cheeses and another clip-lock or airtight plastic food container for ginger, chilli, curry leaves, bits of onion and other pungent ingredients that might contaminate other things in the fridge. Otherwise, before you know it, your raspberries will taste of onion.

- Compartmentalization is key: I have two lidless plastic containers, one for jars of jams, jellies and sweet things and the other for mustards, horseradish sauce, chutneys and savoury things. I find it easier to sort the jars in shallow containers. Storing them like this has the added benefit that you can pull everything out at once, which can be useful at times like breakfast, when everyone wants different jams and marmalades and so on.

- Most modern fridges have a couple of drawers. In theory, I use the top drawer to store salads and the bottom drawer to store vegetables – it's good to keep them separate, as salad goes off more quickly.

CLEANING YOUR FRIDGE

- When you decide your fridge needs a clean is up to you, but it makes sense to overhaul it when there's not much food inside rather than just after you've done a big shop. Take everything out and keep perishables in a cool bag or box (jars and bottles will be fine at room temperature for a short while).

- As with defrosting your freezer, take the opportunity to examine what you have and chuck out anything that's past its best!

- To wash your fridge, take out all the internal drawers and boxes and wash them in warm water with washing-up liquid and a clean sponge. Wipe the interior of the fridge – including the door seals – with fresh warm soapy water. A little

bicarbonate of soda can be used as a gentle abrasive to help shift stubborn stains and spills. Dry the inside of the fridge very thoroughly with a clean tea towel, ensuring the boxes and drawers are fully dry before replacing them.

- Keep your fridge cleaner for longer by getting into the habit of checking that anything that you put into it is drip free. Opened jars or squeezy bottles of condiments are common culprits! (It helps to keep them in a container, see page 24.) If defrosting in the fridge, always place items on a plate to avoid leaks.

- Putting bicarbonate of soda or freshly ground coffee into a plastic container and leaving it in the fridge is meant to help eliminate bad smells, but being vigilant about mopping up spills should mean this isn't necessary.

- If water is condensing on the back wall of the fridge or pooling in the bottom, this can be a sign that warm air is getting in or that the drain is not working efficiently. Check that the door is well-sealed and take any gentle measures you can to remove clogs from the drain, but a persistent problem may require the help of an expert.

WHERE TO STORE PERISHABLES

Food tends to come in a lot of packaging now, much of which is plastic: before storing it, release it from its wrapping so it can breathe. Sometimes vegetables can 'sweat' inside plastic and become slimy.

This is a rough guide, so be sure to check the dates on the packaging.

LETTUCE AND SALAD

Where: Fridge

How long: 2 days

Tip: Dip (or sprinkle) the whole head in cold water, then put it into a bag before storing in the fridge – this will help to keep it crisp.

ROOT VEGETABLES

Where: Fridge

How long: 2 weeks

Tip: Wrap to prevent them shrivelling, before storing them in the fridge.

MUSHROOMS

Where: Fridge

How long: 5 days

Tip: These are best kept in brown paper bags.

GARLIC

Where: A cool, dry place, such as a larder, away from direct sunlight.

How long: Individual cloves can last up to 10 days, unbroken bulbs much longer (so use up the cloves of a bulb you've already broken into first).

Tip: It's not advisable to keep garlic in the fridge as this encourages it to sprout, or in plastic, where it will become moist and rot. A container with holes allowing air to circulate (or something like a wire basket) is the ideal garlic receptacle.

POTATOES

Where: A cool, dark place. A larder is perfect, if you have one, but a cupboard will do.

How long: 2 weeks

Tip: Don't wash potatoes before storing, as they will be more likely to spoil if damp.

BREAD

Where: Ideally in a bread bin

How long: Depends on your bread! Usually between a few days and a week.

Tip: Use up odd ends of bread by making them into croutons or breadcrumbs and freezing.

BASIL

Where: This herb likes sunshine and needs to be kept out in the kitchen, ideally near a window.

How long: As long as you can keep the plant alive!

Tip: Don't put it into the fridge, as the leaves will wilt and turn black. If you have a bunch, not a plant, stand the stalks in a pot of water.

BUNCHED CORIANDER, MINT, PARSLEY, TARRAGON & WATERCRESS

Where: Fridge

How long: 1 week

Tip: Ideally try to buy these with their stalks on (and if they have their roots, even better). Place in a little jug or glass with some water, then put a plastic bag over the top before storing in the fridge. This mimics the conditions of a greenhouse: your herbs will be cool and protected and stay fresh longer.

FISH

Where: Fridge

How long: Try to cook on the same day

Tip: Remove fish from its original packaging, transfer it to a dish or plate, cover it with foil and use as quickly as possible.

RAW MEAT

Where: Fridge

How long: 5 days for large joints, 3 for mince or steaks

Tip: A big joint of red meat will mature in your fridge, so it's a very good thing to buy it 3 or 4 days before you're going to roast it. My mother always used to buy her Sunday joint earlier in the week, when there wasn't a queue in the shop, and keep it loosely covered in the fridge.

EGGS

Where: At room temperature – or keep them in the fridge, if you prefer. Just remember that they will need to be cooked for a little longer if boiling. Allow to come up to room temperature if using for baking or meringue-making.

How long: Follow the date stamp. Leftover egg whites can be kept in the fridge for up to 2 weeks (use for meringues and egg-white omelettes); leftover yolks can be kept in the fridge for up to a week (use for making hollandaise, mayonnaise or curd).

Tips: Store eggs away from heat sources and anything that smells, as they are porous. To test if an egg is fresh, put it into a tall glass of water – a fresh egg will remain at the bottom while a stale one will bob to the surface and float!

THE STORE CUPBOARD

SPICES & SEASONINGS

If you have good-quality cupboard doors, you can fix spice racks to the back of them, which I think is very useful. In our house, I have trained everybody to turn the spice jars round, so you can see what's what. Ideally, all the whole spices should be together, and any baking ingredients kept separately. You may have your own system. Every so often, I reorganize everything: this area is my republic, but certain people come and borrow things without returning them, and don't put the labels facing forward!

Light causes spices to fade and lose flavour,
so they should always be kept in a dark place.

EVERYDAY INGREDIENTS

If you cook frequently, there will be some ingredients that you use all the time: sea salt, cooking salt, black pepper, oil (probably more than one kind), sugar, plain flour . . . It makes sense to have them close to hand, whether on a little tray next to the cooker, or in a vertical drawer.

DRY GOODS

When you're putting food into cupboards, it's sensible to face the labels forward so you don't have to keep turning everything round to see what sort of jam you've got or whatever. I think it looks nicer, too.

Decanting dry goods into glass jars, from flour and sugar, to rice and lentils, is a matter of personal taste. Some people like the way it looks and you can always see exactly what you have left at a glance.

Flour should be used within 4 months once opened.

Fast-action dried yeast, baking powder, bicarbonate of soda, cream of tartar, and any extracts, like vanilla or almond, are best left sealed in the containers you bought them in.

If you are decanting ingredients, it is worth writing the use-by date on a little bit of masking tape or a label and sticking it to the bottom of the jar – otherwise you are sure to forget, especially if it is something you don't use very often. For flour, make sure to write whether it is plain, self-raising, gluten-free, as they all look identical. An alternative method is to cut out the name of the ingredient and the best-before date from the packaging and just slip that into the jar.

CANNED FOODS

Canned foods should be kept in a cool, dry place. Though they last a long time, they do not last for ever, and it's worth checking the use-by dates every so often – a good opportunity to do this is when you empty the cupboard to clean it, as then you need only take everything out once.

Another common sense tip for avoiding having a cupboard full of expired cans is to arrange anything you have multiples of so that the ones that go off sooner are at the front – this way you will use them before cans that have a later expiry date. It might sound obvious, but it's easy to forget! This is something worth bearing in mind when you're out shopping too, as shops (if they are well organized) tend to arrange their shelves in this way.

Avoid buying cans with deep dents or dimples in them, as this might mean that the seal of the can has been damaged and that air has entered it. Avoid bulging cans too, as the contents may not be safe to eat.

Group cans into categories – soups, pulses, chopped and whole tomatoes, fish, fruit, etc. This way it will be easier to tell when you are out of something and need to stock up on it (and you will spend less time scrabbling about if you have deep shelves!).

COVERING & STORING FOOD

All food is better stored wrapped. If you're in a hurry and stick something in the fridge without covering it, it's going to dry out on top or, in the case of salad, wilt.

Both cling film and foil keep smells out and retain the shape of food when folded around it, but each has its place. If you want to be able to see what's on a plate, or in a bowl or packet, cling film is best. It can also be used to cover food being reheated in the microwave, though your appliance's instructions will probably advise you to make holes in it, to prevent it from blowing up into a dome and bursting.

Meat should generally be wrapped in foil, as should anything going into the oven at a temperature over 110°C.

There are different qualities of plastic freezer bag. The more luxurious ones have a zip in the top, which is very good as it can be opened and sealed very easily.

I keep my foil, cling film, baking paper, and different-sized freezer bags together with reusable plastic clips for sealing bags. If you are able to fit a dispenser for both wraps in the kitchen, it's a great help.

There's nothing more infuriating than trying to undo a plastic bag that's been knotted. There are certain people who put knots in the top of bags, but I am not one of them. A plastic clip comes off in a second; when you're in a hurry and you've got to undo a bag that somebody has so cleverly put a knot in, it can drive you mad! Clips are perfect for sealing the tops of opened packets of rice or little grains like couscous, which can go every-where if not sealed correctly. Some people use old-fashioned clothes pegs instead: I remember giving an aunt of mine some plastic clips and her saying, 'Why ever would I need those?' Aunt Jane would close her porridge bags with a clothes peg at the top, so she didn't think my tip was a very good one – but I do!

KITCHEN PLANNING

Whether you are planning a kitchen from scratch, or just want to rearrange your existing one, configuring your kitchen is a very personal thing. Before you even start planning it, think about how you cook and how you will use the space. You are the person who's going to be in the kitchen, after all. It should be practical, or else you'll be cleaning for the rest of your days, so sit down and think about what's important to you. Are you a cook or are you not a cook? Maybe you do a lot of baking, and have lots of special equipment that you need to store. If this is the case, and if your kitchen is a small space where work surface is going to be limited, you may want to factor that in and tuck your food processor and mixing machine away on deep retracting pull-out shelves in cupboards. Or perhaps you don't like modern wall units and you have a collection of plates from your family that you want to show off, so having a dresser is important to you. On the other hand, you might only make stir-fries and eat mainly from bowls, so storing your crockery won't be a priority. It really is a very particular thing, a kitchen. However, it is useful to remember that though there is so much choice available now, at its heart a kitchen is just a room with the sink and cooker in.

A COUPLE OF POINTS TO BEGIN WITH

Are you going to eat in the kitchen? If there's space, then it's quite likely you will. I always like to eat in the kitchen for informal meals – even when we were first married, my husband and I would sit down and eat breakfast together every morning before going off to work.

You've got to have a preparation area and it is best positioned near the sink, fridge and rubbish bin, so you're not running back and forth. Planning a kitchen is about finding a working circle or triangle between these areas, which makes cooking easier for you.

THINK OUTSIDE THE BOX

A kitchen can be any room, as long as it has the essentials in it, and it is wonderful what can be done with a little imagination.

My assistant of nearly 30 years, Lucy, whom I write alongside, has a classic Victorian cupboard underneath her stairs – the kind of space that is often used for stashing a vacuum cleaner and mop, or bulky winter coats and shoes. She transformed it into a baking cupboard by taking the door off, adding shelves and painting the inside. Now it's where she keeps everything she needs for baking, from bulky appliances such as a food processor and stand mixer, to scales, glass jars of flour and sugar, and baking tins and racks. If she is making a cake then everything can be done in there, and all the mess contained, keeping the rest of the kitchen nice and clear. Of course, not everyone has a cupboard under the stairs, or a mixer that needs housing. But just because a space has always been used for keeping a vacuum cleaner in, that doesn't mean that's all it could ever be.

KITCHEN TABLES

If you have the room for it, it's lovely to have a table in the kitchen. Not only is it an area to sit down and eat, but, if you have children, it doubles up as some- where for them to sit and do their homework after school. I found that my children would get up to all sorts of things if they went to their bedrooms to do homework. If they are at the kitchen table you can keep an eye on them!

KITCHEN WORKTOPS

If you are planning a new kitchen, then it is worth thinking carefully about what worktop will suit your lifestyle. More than anything else, it's essential for these much-used surfaces to be hardwearing and practical. Gone are the days when you would have individual tiles on your worktop, because they are grotty, and dirt gets between them too easily. What you need is a smooth surface. Unless you're very fastidious, don't choose black granite, because it smears easily and you'll spend your whole life looking at your kitchen counter, and mopping and polishing it. A lighter-coloured speckled granite, stainless steel or laminate surface is easier to clean, and more forgiving. Granite and stainless steel also have the benefit of being heat resistant. Marble looks beautiful but damages easily and is susceptible to staining. Unsealed wood anywhere near a sink can often be a huge mistake, because you'll continually drop water on it; sealed wood needs a lot of care too, and unless you are incredibly vigilant it will rot and turn black. If you want wood countertops, be prepared to scrub them all the time. It's worth asking yourself, how much work do you really want to put into cleaning your counter?

GAINING EXTRA WORKTOP SPACE

If worktop space is really limited, a wheeled kitchen or butcher's trolley can be a helping hand, especially when plating up meals. The wheels mean it can be used in a variety of places. Ideally, get one with a brake.

If you are designing a new kitchen, you can get worktops that slide in and out of the counter. Similarly, it's possible to build a chopping board into a drawer, so you can just pull it out as and when you need it. An additional section of worktop at the end of the kitchen counter on a hinge that can be securely propped up is also a clever solution.

CLEANING & RESPECTING WORKTOPS

Wipe up spills with a damp cloth as and when they happen; clean surfaces more thoroughly with a cloth and warm soapy water, then wipe dry with a microfibre or lint-free cloth to prevent streaking and damp. Never use abrasive or wire scourers on worktops!

All Worktops

Protect surfaces by using trivets for resting hot pots and pans, and chopping boards for chopping (chopping directly on a hard surface blunts knives and will damage your counter, whatever it's made of. See page 76 for more on chopping boards).

Stone, Wood & Stainless Steel Worktops

Sealing improves the water and stain resistance of stone and wood surfaces though it doesn't last for ever, so it's advisable to reseal – how often you need to do this will depend on how much wear your worktops get.

Oil, vinegar and citrus juice can damage stone worktops even when sealed, and any spills should be mopped up immediately.

Specialist stain-remover sprays and creams are available from all good homeware shops and are very effective for cleaning stone surfaces or stainless steel worktops.

KEEPING A CLEAR COUNTER

Some people prefer machines and appliances to be tucked away, and not taking up work surface, which can be particularly precious if you have a smaller kitchen. I think it's a very good thing to have clean surfaces and not have things out that take for ever to polish – and why should a microwave take up a surface when you can fix it in a cupboard?

If you don't love kitchen wall units, be inventive: an old freestanding wooden cupboard can be used to house bulky appliances, like a microwave, or a coffee machine – you just need to make a hole in the back for the plugs and cables to go through.

It's a good idea to keep your counters relatively clear if you can: unless you are very attached to them, there's really no need for a mug tree – or a banana tree! This can be easier said than done, as things do have a habit of creeping on to the surface and staying there. I find it useful to prioritize keeping open stretches of worktop tidy (in other words, areas without any cupboards over them) where you will be most likely to chop and do other prep work.

KITCHEN STORAGE

COMMON-SENSE ORGANIZATION

If you store things near where they will be used, with the things you use most often closest to hand, you'll save yourself a lot of frustration – this may seem rather obvious but when first unpacking it's easy to put things in cupboards in a hurry and not think about the practicality of what should go where. As with organizing anything, from your living room furniture to your wardrobe, it may take a few reshuffles until you're happy. It's a good idea to keep everyday plates and bowls near the sink or dishwasher (wherever you wash up), so you have minimum walking to do when putting things away. It doesn't make sense to keep everyday plates in a hard-to-reach wall cupboard that you need to get a stepladder out to climb up to every time!

Keep the mugs you use all the time near the tea and coffee and within easy reach of the kettle and the coffee maker. It's all common sense, but worth thinking about. If you have the space, you could even keep everything you need for breakfast in one cupboard, making your mornings simple.

CUPBOARDS & DRAWERS

If you are starting your kitchen from scratch, instead of having cupboards at a lower level and putting things one behind the other, put drawers in. It might not be something you think about now, but when you're older – and I speak from experience! – you won't want to bend down on your knees and be pulling out pans.

- It's very useful to have a vertical storage space – either a cupboard that pulls out or a built-in space with dividers – close to your oven for storing roasting tins, baking trays, chopping boards and things like that. Otherwise, if you store them horizontally in a cupboard, you just know that you will always want to get out the one at the very bottom of the stack! Stored vertically, you can pull them out quickly and with ease.

- It's worth having some shallower cupboards that are the width of your plates so that you can avoid putting things one behind the other, which can be very annoying when it comes to getting out the things at the back.

- If you are able to adjust your cupboard shelves, there's no point in wasting space: measure your tallest glass and make sure the shelf where all your glasses are going to sit is just a little bit deeper than that.

- If you have a lot of mugs, and want to stack them on top of each other, measure how much space that will take and adjust your shelf accordingly.

- If you've got very young children, you may need a whole drawer for plastic mugs, plastic plates, plastic boxes, a bottle sterilizer – all things for littlies.

SHELVES

Wall-mounted shelving is an alternative to traditional wall cabinets, but as everything is out on display, there's nowhere to hide when it comes to mess – or dust! Group similar items such as glasses, plates and bowls together, stacking where you can.

If you want to make a real feature of your shelves and have the room, use them to display any decorative or special items like platters or vases – as you would with a dresser. Line with anti-slip liners for additional security.

A slatted steel shelf on a wall can serve a double purpose: stack items such as pan lids on top of it, and hang pots and pans with a hole in their handle off S-shaped metal hooks. Just take note of the maximum weight it can hold and be careful not to overload it.

Steel rails fixed to the wall near the oven or hob can be used for hanging utensils from S-shaped hooks, freeing up drawer space.

CLEARING OUT & CLEANING CUPBOARDS, DRAWERS & SHELVES

It's good to clean cupboards and drawers every six months; take everything out and use a clean cloth and hot soapy water to wash all the surfaces, drying them thoroughly before you put everything back.

I line my pan drawers with ridged rubber matting; it's durable and gives the pans something to land on – they make marks on the bottom of the shelf otherwise. You can buy it online and from catering companies, and as it is sold by the metre you can cut it to size.

Make a list of your most regularly used equipment and how much you use it – and be honest: if you've not used your cherry-stoner in the last 10 years, chances are you're not going to want it again any time soon. It's taking up space in the drawer where things you do use all the time could go, so put it in a box and label it, then store it in the highest cupboard in your kitchen (or your garage, if you have one). Then, when (or if) you need it, it should be easy to find and take out.

Think of all the things that you use just once a year. Perhaps you make jams and jellies at Christmas-time, and you've got a preserving pan and a strainer for sieving the pulp out of your jelly. Put it out of the way instead of somewhere that's easy to access where you should keep everyday things: a high cupboard or a shelf in an outside space such as a garage or shed. Only store items outside that won't go rusty. I stick to wood and glass.

KITCHEN FLOORING

———————

*People often say that a ceramic floor is hard on the feet, but I don't
find that to be true. Think of those wonderful old ladies in Italy – they've
been brought up on stone floors! If you're planning your own kitchen,
you might want underfloor heating, which is something that should
be decided on initially (it's more expensive to put in later) and
feels very nice, especially in winter.*

———————

If you're having coloured tiles, avoid having the grouting in white – try to match the
colour of the tile. White discolours so quickly: using a darker grout prevents it looking
dirty. This applies outside the kitchen too.

Tiles need to be butted together with minimum grouting: if they are laid badly with
great big gaps between them, dirt will collect on the rough surface of the grouting
very easily, making more work for you in terms
of cleaning them.

See page 110 for how to clean a floor.

KITCHEN SINKS

Whether you have a dishwasher or not, the sink is a main action station and the most important part of the kitchen apart from the cooker.

A one-bowl sink will get the job done, but a one-and-a-half-bowl sink (with a smaller bowl for rinsing veg and salads, or whatever else you want to use it for) allows the sink to work harder. A two-bowl sink is good if you have a lot of washing up or don't have a dishwasher.

Ceramic sinks have a more traditional appearance; made of kiln-fired porcelain, they can chip and crack fairly easily, so take care when placing heavy items on them. Belfast sinks are a classic type of deep butler's sink made of porcelain.

Inset sinks – sinks that are built into the kitchen worktop with a small overlap – generally come with a 'drainer' area for leaving washing-up to dry. You can often choose whether you want this to be on the left or the right, depending on whether you are right- or left-handed, and what you are used to and prefer.

Most sinks are made of stainless steel because it's easy to upkeep and inexpensive: you'll always find it in professional kitchens. Stainless steel does scratch and wear with time, but this is par for the course, and it is easy to clean.

Enamelled sinks are made of heavy-duty cast iron coated in enamel. Avoid leaving anything in the sink that may stain, such as teabags, or using abrasive heavy-duty scourers.

There is an argument for using a plastic washing-up bowl to protect the surface of enamelled and porcelain sinks, although, on the other hand, it may cause markings over time in stainless steel sinks.

TAPS

Taps might seem like a straightforward thing but there are a lot of options to choose from. Most just have one spout and two handles, but some fancy features to consider are high-pressure spray action, a pull-out hose (good for blasting dishes!), and a hot or cold water filter option. If I was planning a kitchen again, I would have an instant boiling water tap, because they are so convenient!

- **Never use abrasive products or scourers on taps as they will scratch. For day-to-day cleaning, wipe with warm water and a little washing up liquid then rinse and buff with a soft cloth to bring back the shine.**

- **Taps are inclined to limescale and mould: use a limescale removal product on chrome or steel taps if necessary, and a specialist mould removal spray if the tile grouting or area around the tap base becomes marked. Keeping the tap and the area around it dry and making sure water doesn't collect can help to prevent both limescale and mould forming, although a sink is inevitably an area that sees a lot of water so it's easier said than done, I know!**

CLEANING THE SINK

According to the NHS, the average kitchen sink contains 100,000 times more germs than a lavatory! That's why it's essential to keep the sink clean and wipe it out regularly.

It's so important to maintain hygiene in the kitchen, and you should keep soap by the sink so you can wash your hands as necessary – usually before and in between handling different types of food. If you use a hand cream, you may like to have a bottle next to the soap.

- **Stainless steel sinks can be disinfected using bleach diluted in hot water.**

- **Use a limescale removal product on any chrome such as sink strainers.**

- **Use something mildly abrasive to clean a porcelain sink: a cream cleaner or bicarbonate of soda on a cloth dampened with a little water.**

- **A specialist cast-iron cleaner should shift stains on enamelled sinks, and can be ordered online.**

Don't pour fat and oil down the sink, as this will cause it to block – and don't I know that! We live in an old house and recently, after Christmas, all our drains outside the kitchen were blocked. We'd had a goose, which has a lot of fat, and I let some go down the sink, which I shouldn't have done. I must say, I really enjoyed unblocking it: I got my rubber gloves, bucket and the drain rods out, and found it very satisfying. What to do with any fat you remove from the pipes? I suggest you take a plastic bottle that has a good screw-top lid, warm any fat, then pour it into the bottle and dispose of it with your rubbish or at a Household Waste and Recycling Centre (see page 85).

If you do have a blocked sink that won't drain, begin by trying the less toxic methods of unblocking:

1. Boil the kettle and pour the water down the sink.

2. Use a plunger to force air through the pipes and dislodge the blockage.

3. Pour bicarbonate of soda down the sink followed by vinegar – they will fizz as they react.

To use drain rods, screw the lengths together as required and insert into the pipe until you can feel the blockage. Push through the blockage in order to loosen it. You may be able to dislodge it at this stage by pouring water down the sink again, but follow the directions on your drain rod for details on how to remove the blockage, as they differ.

If all else fails, use a chemical unblocker: read the instructions carefully, and make sure to wear gloves.

KITCHEN LIGHTING

Lighting is important in the kitchen, not just for being able to see what you're cooking, but also for creating ambience.

Spotlights are very good, especially over the hob, though people often have cooker hoods which have lights in them – very helpful when you're cooking in the evening.

The other main places that should be well lit are the sink, the action stations where you're working and the kitchen table, if you have one. You don't want really bright light when you're eating dinner, so dimmable lights are great for controlling that. The other option is to switch the lights off and have candles, which always seems like a lovely idea, but more often than not you can't see what you're eating, which isn't ideal.

KITCHEN SAFETY

PLUG POINTS

It may seem obvious, but plug points should be high – you don't want them at floor level in the kitchen, as anything you're plugging in will be used at counter level.

Always go for a double socket, if you've got room – if the electrician's going to bother to put a plug socket in, they may as well add two.

FIRST AID KIT

You must keep a basic first aid kit in the kitchen. It is useful for this to contain: a variety of plasters, plain gauze, bandages and sterile dressings, safety pins, disposable gloves, antiseptic wipes and cream, antihistamine, pain-killers such as aspirin, paracetamol and ibuprofen, a thermometer and scissors.

If you cut yourself, disinfect the cut at once, and bandage it up or put a plaster on it straight away.

Don't put ice or iced water on a burn. If you burn yourself, immediately run the area under cold water and keep it submerged, if you can – it takes the air out of it. You used to be told to do all sorts of things, like putting butter on burns, but the main thing is to exclude the air. I once stupidly poured freshly made boiling hot coffee all over my right hand as I was putting the plunger down. It was late at night, so I kept my hand in a jug of cold water for 20 minutes, then I went to bed. For the first part of the night, I just hung my hand over the side of the bed and left it in the cold water. It was quite boring but it did the trick and I had no bad effects whatsoever. If you don't do anything to a burn, it will just keep on burning.

The NHS advises that if the burnt area is larger than the size of your hand, or if it forms blisters, you should go to hospital.

CLEANING & WASHING UP

KITCHEN CLEANING ESSENTIALS

Kitchen cloths: Keep a stash for wiping down counters and other surfaces and wash them daily.

Microfibre cloths: For wiping down surfaces, especially glass-topped ceramic and induction hobs.

Dishcloths, sponges and scrubbing brushes: For washing up – keep separate from any used for other cleaning.

Whitening laundry powder: Use to soak tea towels and kitchen cloths before washing to keep them looking bright and fresh.

Rubber gloves: Keep any old pairs to wear when cleaning the oven, or doing other cleaning around the house. Keep your kitchen pair separate from those you use for cleaning the bathroom, or use different colours for each.

A plastic bowl: Useful when washing up by hand, and it will protect your sink too.

Anti-bacterial spray: A quick way to kill germs and shift stains when wiping down kitchen surfaces.

Cream-based cleaner: Lightly abrasive and good for shifting stains and grease.

Limescale remover: For cleaning taps and steel sinks and returning shine to surfaces frequently exposed to water.

Wire scourers and scouring pads: Be careful what you use these on, as they do scratch.

Washing-up liquid: There are so many different types and scents to choose from now, but everyone has their favourite. Some are more concentrated than others.

Sticker remover: Gets rid of sticky residue on glass jars in seconds, saving you from scrubbing.

Bicarbonate of soda: An effective drain cleaner combined with vinegar, and can be used in place of chemical cream cleaners.

A plunger and drain rods: For dealing with sink blockages.

Dishwasher powder or tablets, rinse aid and salt: Keep your dishwasher in good working condition – use the powder for soaking dirty oven trays too.

Non-stick oven liners: Prevent your oven from getting dirty.

Oven gel cleaner and trays for soaking oven racks: Makes light work of cleaning greasy, stained racks. It's worth shopping around; some are more effective than others.

Polish spray suitable for returning shine to chrome: For cleaning Aga lids.

DISHWASHERS

I couldn't be without a dishwasher. If I were someone with very young children and had a big enough kitchen (and budget), I would like two dishwashers! But that isn't practical for everyone.

- When planning a kitchen, try to position the drawer with your cutlery and the dishwasher close to the table, if possible. You will usually lay the table from the drawer or the dishwasher, so having them near to each other minimizes how much running around you have to do.

- In our house, I insist everybody rinses bits off the plates before they go into the dishwasher. It doesn't take a minute, and I'm the one that cleans out the filter.

- Everyone has their own method for stacking the dishwasher in a way that saves on space, but generally, glasses and mugs should go on the top (placed bottom side up), and heavier items below. Space cutlery out to get the best results.

- Wait until the dishwasher is full before running the machine, as it's much more energy-efficient.

- A good way to clean your dishwasher is to run a wash with white vinegar: around 250ml placed in a container on the bottom rack does the trick – just run a normal cycle and it will be like a new machine.

- My dishwasher has a tray at the top for knives and forks, and every day when I run it, I put the dishcloth and washing-up brush on the top of that tray, to freshen them up. You could also pop the plug from the kitchen sink in there too.

- If your dishwasher gets a lot of action, and there are often different people loading, it's worth sticking a small label on the front with brief instructions about how you want it used. Most machines have a few different wash options, and you will no doubt have a preferred one.

- If the dishwasher's not cleaning properly, it's usually because I've forgotten to put in rinse aid or salt, so do check both those things!

THINGS THAT SHOULDN'T GO IN THE DISHWASHER:

- Cutlery with bone handles
- Cutlery with wooden handles
- Precious knives
- Good glass or crystal
- China with gold or silver detailing
- Cast-iron pans
- Anything wooden (serving spoons, bowls, chopping boards), as it will warp and crack.

If in doubt, leave it out!

WASHING-UP TIPS

- To help keep the kitchen tidy, I try to remember to wash up knives, cutlery and utensils as I'm cooking. I find that an efficient way of doing this is to fill a jug three-quarters full with hot soapy water and stick your dirty knives (blades pointing down) and utensils in there when you're finished with them. Then you can wipe them dry and use them again immediately, saving the time of going to the drawer and getting out another one – and having more washing-up when you're done.

- Pans and dirtier items will benefit from extra time soaking while you wash everything else: squirt in some washing-up liquid and fill with hand-hot water beforehand.

- When washing up by hand it's useful to have a plastic bowl inside the sink as it fills up more quickly, meaning you use less hot water – sinks tend to be so big and if you're just washing a few items it's not necessary to fill them all the way.

- I always keep a plastic spatula close by the sink for scraping plates clean before washing.

- Everyone has their own system, but it does make sense to do glasses and delicate items first when the water is fresh, and leave greasy, large and heavy items until the end.

- Wire scourers or scouring pads are helpful to have for tough cleaning, but should never be used on the outside of stainless steel pans or cutlery.

- If other people are helping you with the washing-up, put the scourers to one side, because they do scratch, if used with pressure.

- Never leave sharp knives or food processor blades in a sink full of water – you can't see what you're grabbing and could easily cut yourself.

- If you're washing up a bowl in which you've made a batter, say, don't use hot water, as this will fix the egg and uncooked flour and make it more difficult to clean: use cold water instead.

- If you run out of space on your dish drainer, or don't have someone on hand to help with the drying-up, a dish drying mat laid out on the work surface next to the sink is a good investment: they are very absorbent, dry quickly and can be easily washed in the machine. A couple of clean tea towels will also do the job.

- The dishcloths, sponges or brushes you use for washing up should be kept separate from anything you use for wiping down surfaces – it's not hygienic to mix them up.

WASHING UP TOUGH THINGS

Stubborn coated-on food in pans and roasting tins: Sprinkle dishwasher powder into the tin, add very hot water and leave to soak overnight.

Burnt caramel: Add a little water to your pan, bring it to the boil, and see the caramel melt into the water.

Brown stains in tea cups and mugs: Caused by the tannins in tea, these should disappear quickly when scrubbed with a scouring pad – or, if you do not have one to hand, rub with salt.

CLEANING

CLEANING LIMESCALE FROM GLASS

Whether it's everyday tumblers or vases, glass products can be prone to limescale, depending on the hardness of the water where you live. We have very hard water, and if you leave a glass of water for a few days, a ring of limescale will be sure to develop around it. If you clean all your glass items meticulously every time you use them, it's almost certain that this will come off eventually, but most of us don't – especially in the case of vases, which are particularly prone to limescale.

Descaling products are very effective at cleaning off limescale. Add a little to hot water, then submerge your glass and wash as normal, focusing on scrubbing the affected area – if you can reach it. Or you could very gently rub a soap-impregnated steel wool scouring pad over it, but be very careful not to scratch the glass. Whichever way, you will find that the limescale disappears.

If glasses or vases have been put into the dishwasher regularly, especially at a high temperature, they will become slightly cloudy, and there really isn't very much you can do about this – I have been told that it's due to lead in the glass. The best advice, though perhaps not always practical, is to wash them by hand in hot water and from time to time add a bit of limescale solvent to the water, to ensure they stay both clear and clean.

Another trick, especially if you have an irregularly shaped glass container, is to add a handful of rice and a good glug of white vinegar. Swirl it around briskly so that the rice can clean all the corners, before rinsing and drying.

If you have stacked glasses that have stuck together, place them in warm water and fill the top glass with cold water.

CLEANING STICKY LABEL RESIDUE FROM GLASS

Empty glass jars can be put to a number of uses (see pages 33, 86, 106 and 263), but some labels can be very tricky to get off, even when given a prolonged soak. And you can ruin your nails trying to scratch them off! (It can also be tempting to try and use something sharp but this scratches the glass – not to mention being a rather dicey thing to do.)

Armed with the right products, your jars can be sticker-free in seconds. Many companies make liquids specifically for removing stickers: soak your jars in hot water first, then peel off the labels and dab on the liquid with the corner of a cloth – the glue should come straight off.

For a homespun alternative, start by soaking jars in hot water with a little washing-up liquid for a few minutes, or until you can peel the labels off. Then, in a small bowl, mix cooking oil (something like vegetable is perfect, nothing expensive or special: save that for eating!) with some bicarbonate of soda so it forms a paste. Dab on to a non-scratch sponge scourer and rub over the sticky area. It should come off easily but, if not, apply more of the paste. Rinse in hot soapy water to get rid of any oiliness and dry.

CLEANING TEA TOWELS & DISHCLOTHS

I wash my tea towels all the time – two to three times a week – though how often you should wash them depends entirely on how much you use them. I soak them in hot water for half an hour with some stain-removing laundry powder to brighten them up, then wash them in the machine at 40°C. Don't forget to wash your oven gloves, fabric hob protectors and aprons too!

Dishcloths should also be washed regularly: you can put them through the dishwasher every day if you have a machine with a cutlery tray at the top. Use them until they get holes (you can transfer them to your car washing bucket then, if you like).

OVENS

Every oven is different and there is so much choice: electric, gas, fan-assisted, range cookers – and that's before you add any fancy features. I hear that a lot of people were rather in awe of the ones on *The Great British Bake Off*, with the doors that slide right underneath.

Get to know your oven: some will be hotter at the bottom, others at the top, some to the right, and others to the left. If you have a range oven, you'll probably find that the smaller oven acts differently from the larger one, proving that even within the same oven things can vary! When you read a recipe, bear the little idiosyncrasies of your own oven in mind, and remember that the timings are there as a guideline, and not set in stone. If a recipe says roast for '20 minutes until it's golden brown', it's the golden brown that is the true indicator, not whether the time specified has passed.

Baking a cake is a good way to test your oven because you can see how it colours. It's something I've done many times: part of my first job at the Bath electricity board showroom was demonstrating how electric ovens worked, and I would do this by baking a Victoria sandwich.

CLEANING OVENS

It's important to keep your oven clean, because a dirty oven will not distribute heat as efficiently – as well as being unhygienic. It's possible to buy non-stick oven liners that catch food spills and can be easily removed and wiped clean, keeping the bottom of your oven grease-free with no need for scrubbing – you can just whip it out and wipe it down before replacing.

- **You can buy trays especially for cleaning oven racks: you submerge them and leave them to soak overnight to get rid of any difficult to budge cooked-on bits of food. I soak my oven racks overnight in hot water with dishwasher powder. The next day I scrub them with a scouring pad and everything comes off.**

- **If I'm cleaning a dirty oven I like to use a gel cleaner, which doesn't require any scrubbing or leave a horrible lingering smell. Paint it on and leave it (how long you do this for will depend how dirty the oven is), then remove with kitchen roll, and wipe off any additional gel with a damp cloth. Whatever product you use, always read the instructions** carefully before you get going, protect your hands with gloves, and make sure the oven is completely cool before beginning to clean it.

COOKER HOODS

- Cooker hoods collect grease and dirt quickly, and as they get sticky dust clings to them. Washable metal filters can be removed and put into the dishwasher or scrubbed in hot water with some washing-up liquid.

- If your cooking hood has a carbon filter, this will need changing fairly regularly (depending on how often you use your cooker). Check your appliance's instruction manual if you're not sure how to remove it.

Cleaning a microwave oven

Put a cut lemon into a bowl of water and microwave on full power for 1 minute – the condensation will release stains around the sides of the microwave, making it easy to wipe clean, and it smells nice too.

HOBS

Whichever fuel type you opt for, when buying a hob it's worth considering how many burners you need – four is typical, but you can choose to have more – as well as the size and power of the cooking zones required, and additional extras such as gas-powered wok burners (useful if you cook a lot of stir-fries) and griddle surfaces.

GAS HOBS

Gas hobs are popular because the heat is visible, easy to control and quick to get going. Some have a safety feature that cuts off the gas supply automatically if the flame goes out, which is reassuring. You can use any type of pan on a gas hob.

- If you find gas hobs a faff to clean, a gas on glass hob may be a good option, though they are slightly more expensive than ordinary gas hobs.

- If you would like the option of cooking on a gas hob, then a single domino hob which can be combined with a ceramic or induction hob may be the answer.

CLEANING GAS HOBS

The stands or supports (usually made of cast iron) and burners can be removed and washed with hot water and washing-up liquid – for any tough, burnt-on spills, use a cream cleaner and/or a scourer, working very gently to avoid scratching the surface.

CERAMIC (ELECTRIC) HOBS

These are more common now than the older style of solid, sealed plate electric hobs, which are very slow to heat up. Ceramic hobs work through a heating element underneath the glass ceramic surface which transmits heat to the hob ring. Heat indicators light up to show when the hob is hot, and indicate when it is safe to touch and clean. Some models may also include child safety locks.

INDUCTION HOBS

An increasingly popular choice, induction hobs work slightly differently from ceramic hobs: copper coils beneath the glass ceramic surface of the hob create a magnetic charge which is transmitted to magnetized pans placed on top of the hob ring. Heat is transferred directly to the pan, so the hob gets hot quickly and is quick to react. The surface of the hob also cools very quickly when a pan is moved off, making them both energy-efficient and safe. You do need to use special pans with magnetized bases on induction hobs, otherwise they won't work!

CLEANING CERAMIC HOBS & INDUCTION HOBS

These are both very straightforward to clean, induction hobs especially, as the fact that they remain cool means that spills don't get burnt on. Wipe the surface down with a damp cloth or microfibre cloth and, when it is cool, use a glass ceramic cleaner.

AGAS

Lucy and I have written in detail about cooking with Agas in *The Complete Aga Cookbook* – and of course we ran Aga workshops from my kitchen for sixteen years! Though there are a large number of different models available today, Agas are all different from conventional ovens: heat is stored in the cast-iron body of the cooker and transmitted to two hotplates on the top, one very hot for boiling, and one cooler for simmering, and two or more ovens underneath, which serve different purposes. To preserve heat and use the traditional model of the cooker most efficiently, the ovens should be used more than the hotplates.

Agas do take a bit of getting used to, as the way of cooking is different, but I find mine such a comfort – not least for the way it makes the kitchen so constantly cosy – and when you know how to get the most out of it, it can make life easier.

- To clean the hot enamel surface, wipe with a slightly damp microfibre cloth – or a regular cleaning cloth and a little bit of cream cleaner. Wipe down often to keep it clean.

- For stubborn stains, cradle a wet scouring pad in a thick cloth: rub hard and spills will come off, but do let the cooker cool down a bit before doing so.

- Use a polishing spray on the chrome lids to keep them shiny. Pads are useful for protecting the chrome lids from scratches when you want to rest pots or pans or other bits on them.

- If the Aga is hot, put the cold plain shelf over the plate to protect your arms and face when cleaning under the lids and use a damp scouring pad.

- Use a wire brush (available from the Aga Cookshop) to brush away any spills around the edges of the plates or in the ovens that have become carbonized.

- The Aga Cookshop sells a little scraper with replaceable blades that's handy for removing stuck-on grime around the lids.

KITCHEN EQUIPMENT

POTS & PANS

Everybody has their favourite saucepans;
a lot of people love their cast iron, but you
can get metal, stainless steel and non-stick.
For me, an ancient old granny, I find cast-
iron pans or casserole dishes far too heavy to
lift up once you've put a whole lot of food
in them, and personally prefer to use
something lighter. I love enamel pie plates
for cooking and use an old one that
belonged to my mother. Metal is a very
good conductor of heat, so enamelware is
especially good for making pies in as you
want the pastry to be crisp underneath,
without a soggy bottom. Enamelware is
relatively inexpensive too.

Aside from working out what suits you best,
the other most important thing to consider
when buying pans is whether they're
suitable for the cooker you'll be using.
Induction hobs, for instance (see page 71),
require special magnetized pans.

- It's worth getting a couple of hardy heavy-bottomed pans, because some can be so flimsy that they buckle.

- Two sizes of non-stick frying pan are good: 20cm and 28cm cover most things.

- Lids are so useful; glass lids are especially good for checking the progress of what you're cooking without disturbing what's in the pan or allowing steam to escape. Measure the size of your pan before it's time to replace it, so that you can buy the same size again and reuse the old lid.

- I like non-stick pans: treat them gently but expect to replace them every couple of years, depending on how often you use them, because they don't last for ever. Remember not to use metal whisks or spoons in them, as these damage the protective coating. How do you know when it's time to get a new pan? That's pretty simple: it won't be non-stick any more.

- If you are very tight on cupboard and drawer space, you can buy non-stick pans with detachable handles that clip on. The pans nestle together, making stacking easy, and you save the space that usually gets taken up by unwieldy handles poking out.

- Whatever you choose, do read the instructions that come with your new pan, so that you can make sure you get the most out of it. Some non-stick pans shouldn't be put in the dishwasher, and some manufacturers recommend oiling their pans lightly after use.

- Traditional woks generally need seasoning before they are used for the first time: if the instructions that come with your pan advise you to season it, it's advisable to do so to get the most out of it. Oil your wok very lightly after washing and drying to keep it in good condition. With any pan that needs oiling, it's good to cover it with a large piece of cling film so that dust doesn't stick to the oiled surface. A wok with a narrow base is not suitable to use on an Aga. Use a 28cm non-stick frying pan which covers the plate instead, to make full use of the heat coming from the Aga.

- A watched pan will boil, eventually, but it will do so much more quickly with its lid on.

CHOPPING BOARDS

Health and Safety would like us to have a specific chopping board for every different thing, and some people prefer to have a range of separate boards for preparing different types of food: green for veg, red for meat, white for cooked food, etc. The choice is up to you. I love wooden chopping boards because they feel more receptive to knives and don't blunt them and, of course, they're natural. I keep scrubbing them, and find that this works well for me. Whatever they're made of, it's so important to give chopping boards a good scrub in boiling soapy water after you use them: I have a special brush for this purpose that I leave upright after use, so that it dries off more quickly.

- If you have prepared food that leaves a stain on your chopping board (fresh turmeric, beetroot and chilli are particularly vicious culprits), try sprinkling it with coarse salt and rubbing this in with the cut side of half a lemon. Scrub as normal afterwards, and repeat as necessary: this should help the mark to fade.

- Most importantly: never put wooden chopping boards in the dishwasher, as it will damage the wood. Plastic boards can be safely washed in the dishwasher.

- Any surface used for chopping should be stable; a wobbly board is no good! To help keep your chopping board secure, use the chefs' trick of placing a square or two of damp kitchen roll underneath the board, at either end.

KETTLES

These days, most people tend to have cordless kettles that have a base that you plug into the mains, but you can also get traditional stovetop kettles that whistle when they boil (these are very good for cleaning suede, as they stay on the boil and keep producing steam).

Though some models have inbuilt filters, if you live in a hard water area your kettle will build up limescale frequently and will need descaling – and if you use it a lot, of course you will need to do this more frequently.

- Descaling solutions are available to buy from supermarkets and hardware stores. Generally, you fill and boil the kettle, then unplug it, add the solution and leave it to do its work – but always read the specific product instructions.

- Shop-bought products are usually made from citric acid: for a homemade alternative, you can add clear/white vinegar after filling the kettle three-quarters full with water and boiling it.

- Descaling your kettle regularly makes it more efficient and extends its life-span, so it's something that is well worth doing.

- If you have a stovetop kettle, brush it out every week with a clean brush and that will just help to loosen the limescale. You have to do it regularly, though.

KNIVES

My kitchen knives are a collection of French cook's knives. I think it's always best if the blade goes through the handle and is sealed with rivets, though knives where the blade is moulded into the handle can work well, too – they can just be more prone to snap. Chefs often use cleavers but I've never succumbed – they feel too large. I'm used to the knives that I've been brought up with, and I'm very happy with them.

Knife blocks
I used to store my knives in the drawer: they could end up anywhere, everybody borrowed them and never brought them back. Someone would want to go and do something in the garden, and my little knives would disappear. It's only recently that I've got a knife block. I rather sniffed at them but they're a very wise thing to have: I know where the six knives that live there are – and my scissors – and everyone in the family has to return them to the block when they use them. I've never been so organized: it works a treat for me, and I wonder why I didn't try it sooner.

Knife sharpening
It's important to keep your knives in good condition by sharpening them regularly. If you're skilled, you can use a butcher's steel – if you are friendly with your butcher, they might even teach you how to use it. I use a chantry knife sharpener, which contains two spring-loaded steels. It's straightforward to use, and can sharpen both smooth and serrated knives.

USEFUL KITCHEN UTENSILS & EQUIPMENT

Baking beans: For baking blind – you can also use dried beans or small dried pasta shapes such as macaroni and reuse them time and again (but don't eat them!).

Colander: Stainless steel is best, as enamel tends to chip.

Corkscrew: Have more than one, as they do tend to disappear. The vertical level sort do the job quickly and easily for those with weak wrists.

Digital scales: Professional scales with the optional addition of a mains plug tend to be the most accurate.

Fish slice: Useful for turning and lifting food. I use a plastic one so it doesn't scratch my non-stick pans.

Funnels: Make decanting liquids easy and mess-free.

Garlic press: Useful to have, although a fine grater also does the job very well – just be careful of your fingers.

Graters: One coarse, one fine (for cheese), one for shavings and one for nutmeg.

Ice cream scoop: A sturdy scoop with a non-stick coating makes spooning out ice cream much easier. Can also be used for portioning cookie dough.

Jar opener/key: If you've ever had trouble opening a jar of honey or jam, this is the gadget for you – clip it underneath the lid of the jar, and it releases the suction and just pings off. If you have an Aga, you can turn the jar upside down and place the lid directly on the heat with great care. As soon as it becomes hot, take it off and undo it. Don't try to open a stuck jar by holding it in a doorway and closing the door on it; it's dangerous and you'll chip off the paint. Been there, done that!

Kitchen scissors: Keep them sharp – they should be sturdy enough to cut through a chicken.

Knives: A range, including one serrated and one small paring (see more on page 77).

Ladles: A small and a large ladle are both useful, but smaller utensils are always best if guests are serving themselves – otherwise the food goes more quickly!

Measuring spoons: An absolute must for accuracy. As a general rule, liquid measurements and anything under 50g are done with a measuring spoon; anything over that should be measured using scales. Unless a recipe states that a spoon is 'heaped', it should be level.

Oven gloves: Whether you have the classic double style, mittens or gloves with individual fingers, keep them clean (wash according to care instructions) and always make sure they're dry before using.

Palette knives: These are essential, and great for lifting things off trays. I like to have three: a big one to get under a cake, a flat one, and a small, flexible one, perfect for spreading butter.

Pastry brush: I like flat ones, as they are much better for getting good coverage. I use clean new paintbrushes, which are cheaper.

Peelers: I prefer a swivel-headed peeler with a handle that is parallel with the blade – you don't necessarily need to spend a lot of money on it.

Potato masher: Whatever shape you like – plastic ones can be used in any pan, while metal may scratch.

Quiche tin: Ideally 28cm diameter and 4cm deep. The loose-based perforated variety are very good.

Rolling pin: I like one without ends, and the longer the better.

Salad spinner: Takes up cupboard space, but makes washing and drying leaves very easy.

Sieves: A small one for dusting icing sugar and flour, a nylon one for fruit (as metal can taint its taste), and a regular stainless steel one.

Slotted spoons: So useful for fishing food out of liquid or for poached eggs.

Spatulas: These have really advanced over the years; I love the pliable silicone sort, which are very good at getting into corners and safe to use in non-stick pans.

Tea towels: A plentiful supply of clean, dry tea towels is a must no matter the size of your kitchen. Use them for drying crockery, glass-ware, chopping boards and anything else that needs it. For tips on keeping them spotless see page 67.

Thermometers: One for meat and one for sugar, jams and jelly-making, and for advanced sugarcraft.

Timer: These days most mobile phones include applications for setting alarms and timers – everything apart from turning the

oven off for you! – but it is always good to have an old-fashioned kitchen timer that is used only for that purpose, as phones do run out of battery and can sometimes be more of a distraction than a help.

Tins: For whatever you like to bake: cake tins in varying shapes and sizes (e.g. sandwich, round, rectangular), loaf, muffin, brownie, madeleine, bundt, Swiss roll tins.

Tongs: Tend to come in two sizes, long and shorter. Indispensable for serving spaghetti and turning things.

Whisks: Small spiral whisks, to get into the corners of pans, and a big balloon whisk (remember that the bigger the whisk, the more air it will get into your mixture and the more quickly).

Wiper cloths: Cotton, sponge or microfibre cloths are handy for mopping up spills and wiping down surfaces. Keep them clean (see page 67 for more on how to wash cloths) and always keep cloths used for washing-up separate.

Wooden spoons: No kitchen can be without them. I like to have a range of different sizes and handle lengths.

Wooden toothpicks and skewers: For canapés and barbecues; also useful for testing if things are cooked through.

LARGER KITCHEN EQUIPMENT

Food mixers are very useful if you do a lot of baking (cakes and meringues, or bread, with the dough hook attachment). They have large whisks, which is why they get more air into your mixture and get it to the desired consistency more quickly than whisking by hand.

Hand mixers are good if space is short, or you don't do much baking.

Food processors have blades for chopping, grating and puréeing. They used to say you could make meringues in the processor, which you absolutely can't, because meringues are all about getting air into the egg whites and when you use a food processor you always put the lid on!

Hand-blenders are brilliant, especially if you are cooking smaller quantities or for making soups, and are generally fairly portable, if space is at a premium.

CUTLERY

A cutlery tray in a drawer is all that's needed to keep forks, knives and spoons neat and separate. Not only will this save you rootling around for the last clean teaspoon, but your cutlery is less likely to become scratched over time. Or, if drawer space is at a premium, keep each different type of cutlery in its own holder or jar for easy access.

Stainless steel cutlery

This is good for every day, especially if you use a dishwasher. I like to use stainless steel cutlery with synthetic bone handles because they are dishwasher safe for a lengthy period of time.

Silver cutlery

There's no point polishing silver if you put it back in the drawer and then when you go to take it out a month later, it's tarnished again! After washing, and rubbing with a silver polishing cloth, I wrap my silver in kitchen paper and cling film before putting it back in the cupboard, because I don't use it all the time. It is only brought out on special occasions and storing it like this ensures it stays shiny.

THE ODDS & ENDS DRAWER

Every home has one, and they normally live in the kitchen. Lucy calls this a 'hope drawer', because it's where you go to when you can't find something, and you think, 'Gosh, I hope it's in here!' Whether it's your glasses, torch, batteries, screwdriver, tape measure or even the odd remote control, it almost always is there.

THE GREEN KITCHEN

RECYCLING

It is so important to recycle rubbish, and it's worth thinking about the easiest and most space-effective way of doing that when you plan your kitchen.

Recycling regulations differ depending on the local council; where I live, we have four recycling bins for different things, and it's very important to me to separate items correctly.

If you are planning your own kitchen, you can choose a sectionalized bin that suits your specific needs and makes recycling simple and space-effective. You can also buy built-in bins to attach to cupboard doors, or free-standing compartmentalized bins.

Usually, your local council should supply different containers for you to recycle in – you may need to request these. They might ask you to separate paper and cardboard, tins and plastics, but the rules will vary according to where you live. It's a good thing to comply with them, and well worth taking five minutes to research online.

It's also worth checking whether you need to wash containers out before recycling them: there is an argument that the benefit of doing this is offset by the water used to do so, but many councils encourage it. Also, from a personal perspective, containers with food left in them will smell and this can be unpleasant! If you are worried about wasting water, you can always use the water left over after you have done your washing-up to rinse out items that you are recycling.

If you're keen on preserving, save empty glass jars, wash them in hot soapy water or put through the dishwasher, and keep for when you want to make homemade jams and pickles. They are also very useful for storing ground or whole spices, and seasonings. See page 64 for how to get rid of stubborn sticky labels.

FOOD WASTE

Most councils supply special bins for food waste. These usually come in two sizes: a small kitchen 'caddy' and a larger outside bin. They may also provide special biodegradable bags on request – if they don't, it's easy to source suitable compostable ones in supermarkets. If you have a food waste container and have enough space under your sink, this is a fairly natural place to keep it.

- Many councils are happy to take raw and cooked food waste, but check your local regulations.

- For what you can use as compost in your own garden, see page 215.

Compost bins come in a wealth of designs and materials that will suit any garden and help you make the most of recycling your kitchen waste.

CLEANING BINS

People are frightfully keen on cleaning their kitchen bins with bleach but it's a waste of product: there's nothing wrong with giving them a jolly good wash with soap and water and then a dry. If you have an outside space, take them out and hose them down.

DISPOSING OF COOKING OIL

Unless you've got a freestanding fryer, I don't recommend deep frying at home. However, even shallow frying can sometimes result in some leftover oil.

Check your council's website for directions on how best to dispose of it: many councils will allow you to add the bottle to your regular rubbish, others may require you to take it to a Household Waste and Recycling Centre, where it can be properly recycled.

You can strain oil after it's been used (wait for it to cool down first), and reuse it. If oil has been used for frying fish it may be best to keep it separate and only reuse it for other fish or seafood. Use your common sense: if the oil smells fishy after straining, it isn't going to be good for cooking doughnuts in!

It's come to the end of its life when it becomes dark in colour, starts to collect bits of food debris and smells. At this stage (again, when it is cool), strain it into a plastic bottle for which you have a lid and secure firmly.

Don't pour old cooking oil down the sink – it can cause blockages!
If you have a blockage, see page 55.

FOOD SHOPPING: BE ORGANIZED

One thing that is terribly helpful in running a home is having a rough routine. It's not a bad idea to sit down on a Sunday night and look at what you're doing the following week, so that when you do a shop, you can think, for example, I'm going to be in four nights this week. That way, if you buy a chicken, the next day you can have cold chicken, then after that a curry, then you can make a soup: it all works out and you minimize waste.

- A memo or notice board in the kitchen (or a magnetic board on the fridge) can be a handy visual reminder to pick up items that you have run out of – if you remember to scribble them down as soon as you notice!

- Of course, as with most things these days, there are shopping list apps that can help with this too – you may well find these useful if you are the kind of person who often writes their shopping list on their phone. You can also share it with your shopping sharer, apparently, so you can both read the same list on separate phones – all very clever, and way beyond me!

- If you do your shopping in person, it's useful when making a list to group items that are sold together (it's easier to do this when you know your supermarket or local shop well), so that you can walk through in a systematic fashion, without having to double back on yourself.

- If you do a regular online food shop, you can take advantage of the feature whereby you 'build' your regular shop, which saves you having to search for items you buy all the time.

WASTE NOT, WANT NOT

When I was growing up, my mum always made something out of nothing; in those days, with rationing, it was very important that nothing was ever wasted.

Stocks

Stock is the happy recipient of many leftover odds and ends, whether it's meat bones or vegetable scraps. When it comes to making meat-based stocks, I don't often have beef bones (and our dog tends to get them when I do) but there are lots of other things you can use to make, or to enhance, a wonderful stock.

- If you roast a chicken – or, indeed, a turkey – keep the carcass and use it to make a chicken stock. Normally chicken carcasses aren't too big, but if you have an especially large bird then you may well struggle to get it into your saucepan. In this instance, it is very useful to freeze the bendy carcass until it's brittle, if you have room. You can store up a few if you like. Bash the carcass(es) with a rolling pin until broken into pieces small enough to fit into your stock pan. The bones will take up less room in the pan, and you can make a more concentrated stock. Alternatively just cut the carcass up with scissors.

- Save mushroom trimmings – any peel or odd ends of stalk – and add those to stock when it's reducing (strain off when it's ready, before using: it gives the stock a lovely mushroomy flavour which is very good when added to casseroles or risottos in particular).

- Root vegetable ends – carrot, celery, onion skins and the tough outer layers of onions that you peel off – will all add extra flavour to your stock (brown onion skins also give it a lovely golden colour). Don't add green leaves, though, as these will make your stock slimy.

Vegetables

When you cook broccoli or cauliflower, don't assume that nobody likes the stalks – I, for one, love them. When you're cooking your broccoli or cauli, put the stalks into the salted water first, to give them a head start, then put the tops in, as these will take less time.

Fruit

- When you have soft fruits that have gone a little bit mushy (whether it's the last raspberries from the garden or black-berry pickings from the hedgerow, or a neglected punnet that's been sitting in the fridge), don't leave them to go mouldy. Give them a new lease of life by putting them into a food processor with some icing sugar, to taste. Sieve the resulting liquid to remove the pips and you will have a lovely coulis for drizzling over cakes, yoghurts, ice cream or cream, or for freezing if you don't want to eat it straight away. Fruit that's just turning can also be a great addition to porridge or for smoothies.

- Squeezed out lemon halves are wonderfully effective when you have stained hands from blackberrying, or from handling beetroot or fresh turmeric: just put your fingers (or whatever bit of your hand is stained) inside the lemon shell and give them a rub round. They are also wonderfully effective natural cleaners and can be used like sponges for wiping down shower doors (see page 105).

Don't throw away vanilla pods after scraping out their seeds: add them to a jar or airtight container of caster sugar, mix together, then leave to make fragrant vanilla sugar – continue to top up with sugar and vanilla pods as and when.

Cooked or prepared food

- Cooking with pastry, you always end up with a little bit left over – particularly with puff pastry. Rather than throwing it away, take the trimmings, roll them out, sprinkle with grated cheese and cut into cheese straws. Bake them in the oven at 200°C/180°C fan/gas 6 for 12 minutes, or until golden, and you have a nice nibble to go with drinks.

- When I make mashed potato, I allow for a potato per person when I'm peeling, and I always seem to have some mash left. The following day, I make bubble and squeak: cook some fresh cabbage, and when it's lovely and bright green, mix it through the leftover potato, season with salt and pepper, and fry it. People love it.

COOKING & BAKING

*This isn't a cookery book or a baking book, though I have
written several of those! But cooking is at the heart of any kitchen,
and over the many years I have been creating and writing recipes,
I have amassed a large number of tips – what follows
is a collection of the ones I find most useful.*

BEFORE YOU BEGIN

- Take the time to read a recipe through properly so that you understand what you have to do and don't miss out on any stages – something that is easily done if you are rushing.

- Make sure you have all the ingredients and equipment to hand before you begin cooking. It can be easy to presume you have basic spices because you saw them in the cupboard a while ago, but physically check to make sure!

- Measure your ingredients carefully and accurately, especially if you are cooking a recipe for the first time. You can experiment by making your own tweaks once you are comfortable with the basic method.

- Metric vs imperial measurements: it is standard to use metric measurements in the UK now, but if you are using an old recipe, you may find that the measurements are in imperial. Use one system or the other, never both. It's worth bearing in mind that US pints and cups are different from those used in countries such as Australia and Canada. If you have to convert the measurements from an American recipe, say, write them down: you may want to make the recipe again (if it turns out well), and doing this will save you the rather tiresome task of converting everything a second time.

- Get out your tape measure and check the measurements of any tins you are using. If the recipe calls for a 28cm tin, use that size of tin – even a small difference in the size of the tin will cause a notable difference in how the cake cooks. This especially applies to a Victoria sandwich: people often say to me, 'My Victoria sandwich never rises,' and they're nearly always putting it into a 20cm tin instead of an 18cm, for example.

BAKING TERMINOLOGY

Creaming describes beating ingredients – most often butter and sugar – together with a wooden spoon or mixer until they're smooth and fluffy. This is what gives cakes their light texture.

Folding is the term used to describe the motion of combining light or airy ingredients, such as whisked egg whites, with a heavier ingredient, such as flour.

Different from stirring, when you fold things together you should use a sharp-sided spoon or spatula and fold the mixture over on itself, repeating this motion gently until the ingredients are combined. The goal is to retain as much air in the mixture as possible.

BUTTER VS BAKING SPREAD

- If you are using baking spread instead of butter and putting it into a mixer for the all-in-one method, use it straight from the fridge – it will have a much better consistency this way.

- Check the label to make sure the baking spread is over 65% fat – any lower than this and the water content will be too high.

- Use butter when flavour is important: biscuits and butter icing are two good examples.

CAKE-MAKING METHODS

Creaming method:

Mix ingredients, most often butter and sugar, together using beaters in a mixer. Then add eggs, little by little, while beating. Add a tablespoon of flour with the final amount of egg, to prevent curdling, before folding in the rest of the flour or heavy ingredients, such as ground almonds.

All-in-one method:

I much prefer this method where you put everything into the mixing bowl together, and I find it gives a very good result.

A very little baking powder can be added (I use less than I used to, as I think there's more raising agent in self-raising flour now) – a level teaspoon per 200g of flour.

The baking spread should be chilled, and the butter must be softened after removing it from the fridge, but if you're in a hurry don't be tempted to use a microwave: this can melt rather than softening it. Instead, cut it into small cubes and put it into a bowl of lukewarm water, then drain immediately: this will make it soft in no time.

If you don't have a mixer, you can still use the all-in-one method, you just need to make sure that the butter is at the right temperature.

If you have a space under the stairs, make the most of it! Fitted cupboards and drawers can make this an ideal storage space.

BAKING TIPS

- Preheat your oven to the right temperature – if you don't preheat it properly, your cake may not rise evenly.

- Don't guess the timings; you need to measure accurately with a digital timer how long you've been baking.

- Make sure you bake in the right place in the oven – the centre is generally best, as the air can circulate fully around the cake here, but all ovens differ, and you will learn where yours is hottest.

- Put your cake into the oven as soon as it's mixed and put into the tin – baking agents start to react as soon as they are combined with the other ingredients in a cake batter, which is why you won't get such good results if you leave it sitting out on the kitchen counter for too long.

- Do grease and line your tins to prevent cakes from sticking. You can buy pre-cut cake liners for all the different types of tins (loaf, springform, etc.), which saves time on cutting them out yourself.

- Close the oven door gently, so you don't push lots of air in when you shut it.

- If you're baking more than one tin at once (for a Victoria sandwich, say), swap the tins round in the latter half of the baking when set and firm, so that they cook evenly.

- Store cakes in a cool, dark place, safely sealed in a cake tin or container – unless they are iced, in which case cover with cling film and keep in the fridge.

COMMON COOKING PROBLEMS SOLVED

Over-salted soups or stews:
A quarter of a peeled potato helps
to take up some of the salt.

**Curdled mayonnaise
(or hollandaise):** Put a fresh egg
yolk into a bowl with a little
mustard, and start again, adding
the curdled sauce to the yolk,
whisking continuously.

Curdled custard or lumpy sauces:
Whizz in the food processor – it
will very quickly recover, with a
bit of luck.

Preparing fish: Skin-on fish can
be slippery when handling, which
is somewhat dangerous when you
are wielding a knife! For a more
stable grip, put a little salt on your
fingers first.

**How much water to use when
cooking rice:** Use the same mug or
cup to measure out your rice and
add double the volume of water to
that of uncooked rice. Allow
approximately 60g of uncooked rice
per person, depending on appetite.

CLEANING & CONFIGURING YOUR HOME

Spit and polish

'There's no sugar coating it: cleaning sounds boring,
but once you get down to it, it's very rewarding –
what's more, if it's done properly it will last.'

When I was seventeen, before I started at Bath College, I went to Pau in south-west France, where my parents had enrolled me on a three-month course at a housewifery school. While I was there, I stayed with a family who had ten children and I remember that the first meal we had was a stew made with horsemeat. I'd left my pony behind at home, and I cried all the way through supper. The other children went to different schools, while I went off to learn to be a good housewife, and I didn't like it at all. The school was a single-storey building and the pupils were made to go outside in all weathers and clean the windows with damp newspaper. It did work – and it was a very good way of getting their windows cleaned – but what a bore it felt at the time.

There's no sugar coating it: cleaning sounds boring, but once you get down to it, it's very rewarding – what's more, if it's done properly it will last. Tackle spring cleaning on a wet day, when you're stuck at home and you've got a bit of time. Even if you only manage to clear out one drawer, it's worth it. Take a moment to stop and look at things that need a bit of attention. Even something as unremarkable as a towel warmer can be made to quite literally shine: we have one in the loo, and recently I noticed that it had somehow got really dirty. So I got a chrome cleaner (see page 127) and cleaned it. Then I looked at it and thought, 'Why didn't I think of that before?' That sums up the experience of cleaning pretty well: once you do it, you realize it's not really so bad, and doing the job properly will pay off in the long run.

Cleaning products have definitely changed over the years and seem to be much milder now. The old loo cleaner that they sold when I was first married was a powder rather than a spray and it was absolutely fantastic at keeping loos clean. It was much stronger: if you spilt it on the carpet, you were in trouble. I still have that original bottle in my cupboard: I kept it, just in memory!

CLEANING: PRODUCTS

If you have the space, it's fairly logical to keep most of your everyday cleaning products in a cupboard under the kitchen sink but if you have young children or pets in the house, then they should be child-locked or made absolutely inaccessible to small hands or paws.

Organize your products into groups: it's helpful to have all your bathroom cleaners together, then your kitchen products, and any sprays and potions for cleaning carpets or getting out stains. Separate them into polythene boxes, and put the cloths that you use for, say, cleaning the shower or dusting in there too. A smaller, deep box is more practical than a very wide one, both in terms of making the most of your cupboard space, and because then you can grab everything you need in one go and carry it with you, without having to make trips back and forth.

I always like to try to keep a spare of each product, because I'm made that way, but this is only practical if you have the room to store everything together (if it's not immediately visible, you might end up forgetting what you have already stocked up on . . .).

ESSENTIAL CLEANING PRODUCTS

A liquid spray cleaner – check that your bathroom cleaner doesn't do the same job as your kitchen cleaner – you only need one limescale remover spray, for example.

A cream cleaner – these are slightly abrasive, so are good for stubborn stains that need a little more work.

Polishers and dusting cloths – keep separate ones for the bathroom and kitchen.

Bleach – take care when using this, as the fumes are powerful and the liquid can take the colour out of fabrics.

Absorbent kitchen roll – for blotting and mopping.

Bin liners – if you like, you can reuse your supermarket or other plastic bags to line your bins. Every room needs a bin for tissues and things like that. Look out for biodegradable bags.

An old toothbrush – for cleaning grouting and nooks and crannies in doors and cupboards.

Cotton wool buds – these are excellent for getting into hard-to-reach corners, like indented detailing in kitchen or bathroom cupboards.

HOMESPUN PRODUCTS

Good cleaning products need not be expensive, and you might already have them in your cupboard.

Bicarbonate of soda

This is incredibly effective for a number of cleaning jobs around the house, and is mildly abrasive too, making it a good alternative to chemical cream cleaners.

Clear vinegar

Vinegar is efficient at cleaning glass when diluted slightly.

Lemon

Squeezed-out lemon halves are also good for glass, and well worth saving for cleaning the shower: rub on glass doors and chrome fittings to remove cloudy stains and bring back shine.

Lemon and bicarbonate of soda

Combined together, lemon and bicarb are effective for cleaning chrome and anything that needs buffing up.

FRUIT VINEGARS

If you want to clean with vinegar but are worried about your house smelling like a fish-and-chip shop, then why not try a fruit-infused alternative.

· 1 ·

Pour clear vinegar into a glass jar until three-quarters full.

· 2 ·

Add the peel of a citrus fruit (such as lemon, lime, orange or grapefruit) and a few sprigs of mint or a cinnamon stick – whichever combination you find most appealing.

· 3 ·

Leave it in a cupboard to infuse for around a month.

· 4 ·

Use a strainer to extract the scented vinegar liquid and pour it into a fresh jar or empty spray bottle.

GENERAL CLEANING

DUSTING

Dusting is something that my mother always used to do when she came to stay with us; older people are often worried by dust, though I'm not, really – but I do like everything to be clean. The important thing is to find the right tool for the task.

TRADITIONAL DUSTERS

Whoever invented thick cotton dusting cloths and made them yellow has a lot to answer for. The number of times one of those traditional yellow dusters got in the wrong wash when I was first married and all our whites turned yellow . . . For this reason, I am not a fan. You can get white versions, and how sensible is that – I've always got a stock of them. Though very good, cotton dusters are not always lint-free, and for this reason, perhaps, microfibre cloths are increasingly popular for dusting and wiping.

DUSTING BRUSHES

Small soft-bristled brushes are brilliant for dusting across the tops of books, where dust tends to accumulate, without damaging them.

LONG-HANDLED DUSTERS

Long-handled dusters are good for reaching dust and cobwebs in high corners: ceilings, cornices, picture frames, light fittings . . . they come in a range of lengths (some with extendable handles for very high ceilings) and can be made from a variety of materials.

All dusters should be given a good shake outside after use. When this isn't going to cut the mustard, and you have an ostrich or wool duster that needs more intensive cleaning, submerge it in lukewarm water with a little washing-up liquid in it, soak for a couple of minutes, then swirl around. Rinse it in clean water, then gently squeeze out excess water (you can also give it a little shake to help with this), hang it upside down and leave to dry naturally. Feather dusters might need a little fluffing up by hand after this treatment.

Ostrich feather dusters: The classic duster. The feathers are a natural by-product and are traditionally used because they develop a static charge which helps to attract dust. Their delicate nature also makes them ideal for dusting precious or fragile items.

Wool dusters: These are made from natural materials, which is something that is important to many people now, and are good at picking up dust while also being gentle.

Synthetic and microfibre dusters: Very popular now, these often have removable heads that can be washed in the machine (check the label for specific instructions), and replacement heads can also be purchased for when they're past their best.

DIY duster: Wrap a dusting cloth around a long-handled broom and secure it with an elastic band or similar.

MICROFIBRE CLOTHS

Unlike some cotton cloths, microfibre cloths don't leave any lint or fluff behind after use. They are made from very fine fibres (480,000 fibres per square centimetre, in fact!) and are designed to be used with just a little water – meaning you don't need to use chemical products. They can be machine-washed when in need of a refresh, or simply rinsed and wrung dry when you're done.

CLEANING CARPETS, RUGS & FLOORS

CARPETS

Carpets are rather out of vogue at the moment, but they do help to absorb household noise, if that is a concern, and can be easily cleaned.

Carpet stains – like all stains – are best dealt with immediately, or as swiftly as possible, using a stain remover specifically designed to be safe for use on wool and upholstery.

1. First, if wet, blot any excess liquid with kitchen roll or an absorbent clean, colour-fast cloth.

2. Spray or apply the stain remover as per the directions.

3. Blot the stain with a clean cloth or kitchen roll (it saves on the washing), and repeat as necessary.

If wax has got on to a wool carpet, place kitchen roll or greaseproof paper on top of the affected area, then iron it. The wax will melt and stick to the paper. Take care with synthetic carpets as they don't take well to heat!

DEEP-CLEANING CARPETS

While vacuuming is effective, deep-cleaning removes ingrained dirt and dust and extends the life of carpets. It's not something that needs to be done regularly, but it is certainly worth thinking about occasionally, in the same way that you might have the outside of your windows professionally cleaned – or when your carpets have suffered from a period of wear and tear (having building work done, for example, or a large party).

Professional carpet-cleaning machines use a vibrating brush to disturb deeply lodged dirt. They are available for hire from DIY shops, dry cleaners and supermarkets across the UK (check their websites for specific details) and come with their own detergent – all you need to add is hot water – and you can even get them delivered to you.

If you are hiring a professional carpet cleaner, prepare ahead and be sure that you have someone to help you move furniture out of the way. Vacuum carpets to remove any surface dirt before you get going, as this is meant to help the machines work more efficiently.

PROTECTING CARPETS

If you're having a serious party and there's a hallway or area that you know lots of people are going to be walking through, then, depending on how important your carpet is to you, you might consider investing in the rolls of polythene film that builders use to protect flooring. It is very tough and works a treat at protecting your floor from scuffs and spills.

Do make sure to buy the appropriate film for your flooring: the one meant for carpet shouldn't be used on wooden or other hard floors, as it'll never come off!

RUGS

Like carpets, rugs should be regularly vacuumed to ensure they are dust and crumb-free (and to deter dreaded moths – see pages 188–9). Depending on their size, rugs can also be taken outside, if you have outdoor space, and beaten to get extra dust out. Leave them over a washing line (or clean garden table) to air for a couple of hours before replacing. If they are situated in an area that gets a lot of direct sunlight, it may also be worth considering turning them every few months so that they fade more evenly.

Valuable rugs should always be deep cleaned by a professional (though, unless the rug in question is very valuable, the same principles for removing stains apply as for carpets, see page 110).

VACUUMING

A good vacuum cleaner is worth its weight in gold. Depending on the type, vacuum cleaners usually come with a range of different attachments for the retractable vacuum tube.

Whether it's cleaning a keyboard, a sofa or a mattress, use these attachments for the specific tasks they are designed for: they are meant to make your life easier.

- **Upholstery brushes: for cleaning upholstered furniture, curtains and blinds.**

- **Soft dusting brushes: for delicate surfaces (such as the tops of books and picture frames) and vents.**

If you have a lot of carpets and more than one floor in your home, consider keeping a small or older model upstairs (ideally something light and rechargeable – see cordless vacuum cleaners, right).

UPRIGHT VACUUM CLEANER

- The traditional model: good for cleaning large areas.

CYLINDER VACUUM CLEANER

- Lighter: good for manoeuvring.

- **Takes up less room** when stored.

CORDLESS OR HAND-HELD VACUUM CLEANER

- Handheld models are small and light: good for cleaning smaller areas.

- Cordless models run off battery power so you don't have to be near a plug point.

- **Quick and easy** to use.

Whatever type of vacuum cleaner you have, bagged or bagless, empty the bin or replace the bag frequently to ensure that the machine works efficiently.

FLOORS

Our kitchen sees a lot of activity with dogs – and people – walking across it all the time. I use a steam mop to clean my tiled kitchen floor and I don't think it's too much to say that it's changed our lives, especially when you think of all the fancy cleaners we used to try.

Steam mops are quick to heat up, can be used on any sealed floor surface, and the reusable microfibre pad collects dirt with minimum effort, leaving your floor safe and germ-free. And yes, they really do only use water – and leave the floor dry. They really are absolutely brilliant. In terms of storage, they aren't too bulky, so they don't take up very much room, and the pad can be easily removed and washed in the washing machine with all your other cloths.

If you prefer a traditional mop made of string, cloth or sponge, make sure to dry the mop head upright. Hot soapy water (use a little washing-up liquid) should do the job. Be sparing if using commercial floor cleaning products, as too much can leave a rather sticky residue.

WOODEN FLOORS

A dustpan and brush (or the soft brush attachment on a vacuum cleaner) will help you keep on top of the dust and fluff that tends to accumulate in the corners of wooden floors. Vacuum cleaners may mark wooden floors if not used very carefully – follow the instructions according to your particular floor: some wooden floors are sealed, some aren't, and how you should care for them will differ accordingly. You can also buy spray mops to use with specialist cleaning products.

A lot of polished wooden floors require polishing and you can hire a heavy-duty polisher for occasional cleaning.

CLEANING WINDOWS, GLASS & MIRRORS

Use whichever glass surface cleaner suits you – all you need is something that does the job without leaving streaks. A half and half mixture of vinegar and water is a traditional window-cleaning solution and an alternative to chemical sprays; some branded cleaners advertise the fact that they contain vinegar!

As mentioned, when I was studying in France we cleaned windows with screwed-up wet newspaper, which was very effective, though the print does come off on your hands, so it's a good idea to wear gloves – save ones that are no longer useful for washing-up for this purpose.

It's straightforward to clean the insides of windows, unless they are very tall – how often you need to do so will depend on the room in question. Bathroom and kitchen windows tend to get steamed up more frequently, meaning that they need cleaning more often.

If you have very tall windows and struggle to clean them even with a ladder, it's often easier (and safer) to get a professional window cleaner to come and do the bits you can't reach and the outside. Interestingly, many window cleaners now bring their own water, and have their own special methods . . .

How often you will need to do this is up to you and depends on where you live, and how often it rains. Usually it's just before you have visitors coming – or when the sun comes out and you realize that you can't see through the windows.

LIGHTS

Light fittings need regular dusting and a long-handled duster is probably the most sensible thing to use for the job. If you've got to get up on a ladder or a pair of steps to do it, make sure there's somebody around to hold it steady while you do so. The same applies for changing lightbulbs.

- **Note down which types of bulbs you need – bayonet, screw or halogen and the wattage – and make sure you always have a couple of spares so you don't get caught out.**

Lamps and lampshades should be cleaned regularly using a vacuum attachment or a slightly damp microfibre cloth.

CLEANING PAINTED WALLS

If you're planning to repaint your walls, it's worth investing in a good-quality paint that is washable, wipeable and stain-resistant, as so many now are. This is especially important in areas of the home that get a lot of traffic, such as hallways.

To clean painted walls, simply wipe gently with warm water with a little washing-up liquid in it, using a clean, colour-fast cloth or sponge – if the paint isn't the washable sort, then choose an inconspicuous area and start by rubbing very lightly, checking the cloth to make sure that the colour is not coming off. When you're done, blot the area dry with kitchen roll or a clean cloth. It's best to try to clean marks as soon as you notice them.

If you have newly painted walls you can counteract the smell by cutting two onions into quarters and leaving them cut side up on a plate overnight: they will neutralize the smell of the paint – without making the room smell of onion! I got this tip from a friend, and when I asked our painter about it, he said it really worked.

CLEANING WOOD FURNITURE

Dust furniture with a microfibre cloth or duster.

Some **spray cleaners** may be unsuitable for use on unsealed wood, so always read the instructions.

Polish non-precious furniture and woodwork with a wax-free spray to bring back the shine – wax attracts dirt and dust, which then stick to the wood.

Antique furniture should be cleaned with caution: wiping with a just damp soft cloth (or using dampened cotton wool buds for hard to reach areas) is unlikely to do any harm but it's advisable to ask for advice on how best to clean items when you buy them.

Keep wood furniture polished to **prevent stains**.

Sticking drawers: If you have drawers that are difficult to open, ease them out and rub the bottom with a layer of candle wax.

Treating scratches: break an oily nut, such as a walnut, in half and rub the exposed area over scratches in the wood. The oil of the nut should help them to fade and appear less noticeable.

GENERAL HOME ORGANIZATION

CLUTTER & DECLUTTERING

As with the kitchen, I like the surfaces around the rest of the house to be kept fairly clear, if possible. Of course, I have objects that I enjoy looking at – vases and jugs, framed pictures and so on – but I am reasonably tidy and try not to have things that get in the way. That said, there are times in life when clutter is unavoidable – such as when you have young children.

I do have corners where I allow myself to collect various bits, such as a drawer where I keep things that I haven't yet had time to read or gifts that I need to say thank you for. I suppose this drawer acts like a filing tray: when I open it I know that I ought to be doing something with anything that's in there! You will know best what is achievable for you, but having designated areas – whether it be a drawer, box or cupboard – where you allow the paraphernalia of day-to-day life to accumulate is certainly one way to cope without letting clutter take over, though you will have to deal with the things eventually.

DISPOSING OF FURNITURE & BULKY GOODS

It is so important to dispose of unwanted large items responsibly. Leaving furniture or electrical goods on the street is 'fly-tipping' and carries a fine, apart from being lazy and very offensive!

Some charity shops will gratefully receive furniture that is no longer needed, provided that it has a fire label, if upholstered, and is in good condition (i.e. clean, without noticeable damage); they may even be happy to pick it up from you. Otherwise, you can arrange for your local council to collect unwanted large furniture, some white goods, and electrical equipment for a small fee. The number of items councils will collect and how much they charge does vary, so again this is something that it is worth checking online.

Your council may well find a way to reuse your items, but I am told that there are also not-for-profit websites such as Freecycle, where you can list furniture and electrical goods and donate them to someone who is looking for just the thing you no longer need! Of course, there are many more sites where you can list your items for sale, if you feel they have some value.

ROOMS OF THE HOUSE

THE BATHROOM

Apart from the kitchen, the bathroom is my favourite room of the house: we are lucky to have a lot of storage space and it is a great luxury. However, even if you have a very small bathroom, it's worth making it a clean and tidy domain.

MIRRORS

Most bathrooms have a mirror above the washbasin or fitted on the door of a cupboard, but a double-sided mirror with a magnifying side and an extendable arm is always a very practical choice – it helps with putting on make-up!

Wherever the mirror is, it's very useful to have a bright light nearby for shaving or plucking, or whatever else you want to do.

BATHROOM STORAGE

Whether large or small, all bathrooms need some storage space. I have come to the conclusion that a shallow wall-mounted bathroom cupboard is a huge joy. If the shelves inside are narrow, you can't double-stack your jars and potions, and you can see everything easily – no more scrabbling around, or forgetting what you have.

TWO-PIN SHAVING SOCKETS

Electric sockets in the bathroom should, for obvious reasons, be avoided – but two-pin sockets are useful to have for shavers and rechargeable electric toothbrushes. It's not advisable to plug anything else into them.

CLEANING BATHROOM MIRRORS

These get more steamed up and therefore more dirty than mirrors in other areas of the home, so they need more frequent cleaning. Scrunched-up newspaper and a solution of diluted vinegar work well (see page 117), or you can use a window- and glass-cleaning spray and a microfibre cloth that doesn't leave bits of lint on the surface.

MEDICINE CUPBOARDS

We have our medicine cupboard in the bathroom. This may seem a natural place for it, but really it depends on your bathroom and how well ventilated it is, as it is important that medicines are kept away from heat and steam and moisture, which can prevent them working as they should. If there are young children in the house, having a lock on the medicine cabinet door makes sense; a spot that is cool, dry and high enough to be inaccessible to little hands is ideal.

It's a good idea to keep a first aid kit in the kitchen too (see page 57).

- Keep medicines in their boxes, along with their original instruction leaflets (read these to check whether they need to be stored in the fridge).

- Medicines do go out of date, so it's worth sorting through everything now and then. There's always someone in the house who puts back an almost empty bottle of cough syrup, or a box with one lone plaster rattling around in it, so having a clear-out is a good opportunity to see what needs restocking. The NHS advise that you should not throw expired medicines in the bin, or flush them down the loo – take them to your local pharmacy instead, so that they can dispose of them carefully.

- I like to store everything in plastic baskets roughly grouped by type of medicine, as this makes it easy to find what you need quickly. What you keep depends on your individual needs – and if you have children, you will probably find you need a whole lot of additional things. I organize mine as follows:

  Pills and powders: Painkillers such as aspirin, paracetamol and ibuprofen, rehydration salts, antihistamines.

  Things for eyes, ears, skin and feet: Antiseptic creams, ointments and drops.

  First aid items: Gauze, dressings, bandages, plasters, a pair of tweezers for removing splinters and a digital thermometer.

  Holiday creams and medicines: Sun screen, insect repellent and bite cream or gel.

LOOS

We live in an old house which is problematic when it comes to cleaning loos and sinks, because of the hard water stains. If you live in an area with soft water then this won't be such a challenge for you, but all loos need to be given a thorough clean.

- First of all stick on your rubber gloves to protect your hands.

- Flush the cistern, and then remove a mugful of water from the bowl – I use a tin mug. You should be able to see the rim of the limescale line clearly now.

- While the water level is low, pour, brush or spray the loo cleaner around the limescale in the bowl. Make sure you get the product around the top, and where the water drips down the back of the bowl, too.

- Leave for 30 minutes (or according to the instructions on the product label), then rub with a fine scourer or brush. If you have hard water and a lot of limescale, you may need to add extra product.

- Pour the water in the mug back into the bowl, then brush and flush the cistern again.

> *I keep the sponge and tin mug I use for this job in the cupboard in the bathroom – and make sure that it's not used for anything else!*

SHOWERS

If you can, a good habit to acquire after taking a shower is using the handheld showerhead extension (if you have one, if not detach the showerhead) and spraying the walls and door of the shower cubicle to get rid of any suds. Run a squeegee (a rubber-edged blade like those used by window cleaners) over the walls and door to get rid of excess water and prevent unsightly water marks and mould forming.

Spray walls and fixtures with a limescale remover to remove hard water deposits.

If your showerhead is above a bath, a non-slip mat is a good idea and a machine-washable one is especially convenient. If the mat can't go in the machine, give it a good scrub in warm soapy water and leave to air dry.

Plastic shower curtains can usually be put in the washing machine too: check the label. They should be washed regularly, otherwise they can become mildewy.

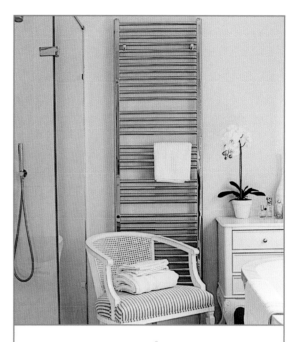

TOWEL WARMERS & RAILS

The best thing to use to get rid of marks on chrome items such as towel warmers is a metal polish cream. If you have something made of chrome, it's nice to keep it shiny.

EXTRACTOR FANS

Good ventilation is so important in a bathroom, and extractor fans need to be kept clean in order to work efficiently. Use the dusting brush or nozzle attachment on your vacuum cleaner to remove dust build-up, then wipe clean.

BATHS

As with the shower, give the bath a good rinse after every use – and encourage everyone else in the house to do the same. This prevents dirt building up and makes life easier. Using bath oils or bubbles can leave behind dirty-looking rings, in which case, rub very gently with a mildly abrasive cleaner (check that it is suitable for your bath first – a plastic bath will scratch) or a little bit of bicarbonate of soda made into a paste with a few drops of water.

WASHBASINS

A simple wipe down with a cloth (keep one in the bathroom just for this purpose) and some warm soapy water should do the job day to day. A mildly abrasive cream cleaner can be used more occasionally, but don't use anything harsher than this or it could damage the washbasin.

BLACK MOULD

This has an unpleasant tendency to build up on white grouting in areas that stay damp, such as shower corners or, if you have tiles, by the edge of the bath. It can be very difficult to get rid of with regular cleaning products that you buy in the supermarket, but some of the specialist mould removal products out there can be very good. Follow the individual product directions: these usually involve applying the spray to the affected area and leaving it to work before rinsing off. Reapplication may be necessary if the mould is severe, but there is no need to scrub! It's advisable to cover your mouth and make sure the bathroom or surrounding area is well aired, as these products can be quite strong-smelling.

Easier said than done, I know, but if you can, try to avoid collecting too many shower gels and other bottles around the edges of showers and baths, as these are a breeding ground for nasty black mould and mildew. If you have half a bottle of shampoo that's been lingering at the side for months because no one likes it, be ruthless and chuck it out!

THE BEDROOM

Bedrooms are all about beds, and it's worth investing in a good one – see page 153 for more on this. Otherwise, this is a room where you go to switch off and sleep, so you don't want too much clutter.

BEDSIDE TABLES & LIGHTS

It's funny, but when you go away, whether it's to stay with friends or to a hotel, you suddenly come home and think, 'Oh, wasn't it nice having a table by the bed with room for a lamp and a book – maybe I do need one.'

Most of us want to read in bed, and to enable you to do so it's a good thing to have an independent light (i.e. not the main light in the room) that's reasonably bright and that can be angled.

As well as being a place to place lamps, bedside tables are useful for stashing books, alarm clocks, radios, torches, earrings, face creams, medication, reading glasses, eye masks, earplugs, tissues, notepads and pens, glasses of water, or whatever else you like to keep by the side of the bed. If you like a lot of reading material to hand, a table with a shelf underneath might be good. Or, if you're short on space, you don't have to use a conventional bedside table: a stool or basket works well too.

MIRRORS

If you have the room, a mirrored dressing table will free up the bathroom mirror, and is, of course, a good place for storing make-up, jewellery and toiletries.

Full-length mirrors are essential too, for checking that the length of what you're wearing looks right, or any other number of outfit-related dilemmas! If you can't have a free-standing one, very often you can fit one on the back of a wardrobe door – or even have it in the bathroom, though it will get steamed up there.

LETTING IN AIR

It's nice to open the windows first thing in the morning, pull the duvet down and let the bed linen and room really air for half an hour or so every day (while you have breakfast, perhaps), even though this can feel counter-intuitive in winter.

KEEPING OUT LIGHT

Everyone is different, but
many of us would agree that
it's fairly essential for the
bedroom to be blacked out.
Not such an issue in winter,
but you don't want the
summer sun coming in and
blinding you first thing in the
morning. Blackout blinds are
a good idea and can go
behind curtains, if you like.
Made-to-measure shutter
blinds are also very effective.

THE LIVING ROOM

Let what you enjoy doing in the living room dictate the layout of your furniture. If you have a fireplace, this is a traditional focal point around which to arrange your seating. Otherwise, a television is often a natural centrepiece.

However you arrange your seating, it's good to ensure that there are surfaces nearby for placing glasses or mugs, so guests don't have to resort to perching them on their lap or the floor.

Lighting is also important: whether the main light is a singular ceiling light shade or a number of small halogen ceiling lights, a dimmer switch is a good thing to have. Floor or table lamps positioned throughout the room also create a cosy atmosphere and allow the room to be used for more than one purpose – so one person is able to read while someone else watches a film, for example.

SOFAS

A sofa is a sizeable investment and, providing you take care of it, should last for a good length of time.

The first thing anyone tends to think about when choosing a sofa is how it looks. Do you want a shape that is modern and sleek, or more traditional and rounded, and what fabric and colour will be best? While you may love pale pink velvet, you probably should ask yourself, is it practical with my life? If you have small children or pets, or like to hold drinks parties, lighter colours may not be such a good idea!

Everyone's definition of comfort is different and, as with mattresses (see page 156), some people may prefer a soft or a firm feel. Do you want to sink into your sofa, or feel more supported? It's a good idea to try them out in person, if you can.

Generally, sofas stuffed with feathers are softer and have a less rigid, more informal look. A fibre- or foam-filled sofa will have a firmer feel, and is good for those with allergies.

Whatever material you choose, durability is important – this applies to armchairs too.

Cotton and cotton blends – Versatile and hard-wearing. Covers can usually be removed and dry-cleaned (follow the instructions on the label).

Linen and linen blends – Can have a textured look. Covers can usually be removed and dry-cleaned (follow the instructions on the label).

Velvet – Will develop a crushed appearance over time. Avoid getting it wet.

Wool – Warm and cosy but may bobble.

Leather – Can be sealed or unfinished. Easy to keep clean by wiping it with a slightly damp cloth. It will crease and age with time, but this is part of its charm.

Loose covers can be removed and cleaned – good if you have young children or pets and are worried about stains and spills. It's worth keeping a spare set.

SOFA & SEATING ACCESSORIES

Throws and blankets are very much in fashion at the moment, and are jolly useful for throwing over yourself when it's chilly. If you have pets, and they are allowed on the furniture, placing a blanket on their favourite spot is a good way to protect the surface from grubby paws and fur.

Small side tables and reading lamps positioned beside chairs and at the end of sofas are very useful if you are fond of reading – a bright overhead light can be rather harsh in the evening.

SOFA SIZE

The scale of the sofa compared to the room you want it to sit in is something to think about. If you have very high ceilings, a low-backed sofa may appear lost in the space; conversely, if the room is on the snugger side, a large and high-backed sofa may dwarf it. These are obvious points, but it's worth considering them rather than realizing too late that you have made an expensive mistake.

If you don't have a spare room, but might need to accommodate house guests sometimes, a sofa bed is a much more practical option than fiddling around with inflatable mattresses, which always seem to have a puncture whenever you get them out, no matter how carefully you treat them.

Size is crucial for another reason: you need to work out whether the sofa you want can be transported through your home to where it needs to end up. Don't just measure the space in which the sofa will sit: doorways (the front door and all other doorways it must pass through), stairs and hallways all need to be considered too. You don't want to order something only for it to get stuck! If space is tight, a sofa with detachable legs and arms may be a good option. Corner sofas often come in two parts which can be fitted together.

Whatever its size and shape, a sofa should have some form of castor to make it mobile, as you will have to move it to clean behind it every few months.

SOFA MAINTENANCE & CLEANING

Positioning your sofa so it sits in direct sunlight may cause the colour of the fabric to fade, so it is best to avoid this if you can. Try to avoid placing a sofa right up against a radiator too – not only can this damage the material, but it will prevent the heat spreading efficiently throughout the room.

Loose cushions need plumping – especially those filled with feathers. Give them a vigorous beating and a shake every day, if you can. Rotate the pillows regularly to ensure that they wear evenly.

Many retailers offer a fabric (or leather) protection service provided by external companies at an additional fee. This generally involves your furniture being pre-treated before delivery, and support and cover should you suffer any particularly vicious stains. If you would like to purchase fabric protection, it is worth checking that the product applied is not harmful in any way.

Use the upholstery attachment on your vacuum cleaner to regularly remove dust from sofa surfaces and dust and fluff from underneath cushions.

COFFEE TABLES

Coffee tables tend to be surfaces that get a lot of use: they are a resting place for drinks and snacks, candles, flowers, magazines, books, remote controls, trays – and sometimes feet! (We no longer have ashtrays because, very sensibly, everybody seems to have been giving up – or they suddenly have a great interest in the garden and go for a little walk, and come back all smiles.) It is therefore important that a coffee table should be fairly sturdy and certainly stable. Begin by thinking about how you will use the surface. The way we eat is much less formal now and, if you don't have a kitchen or dining table, the coffee table may also double up as an eating and entertaining space.

- **A table with a shelf is a good option if storage is an important consideration.**

- **If you like modern furniture, or want to create an illusion of space, a glass coffee table can be attractive. However, the combination of sharp-edged glass (or indeed any low-standing sharp edges) and small children can be a dangerous one. Some people pad out the edges of their tables with foam bumpers, to 'baby-proof' them, but** whether or not to do this is up to you, and it may be easier to simply have a table that poses less of a risk!

- A pile of easily visible coasters is a good way to protect unsealed wooden tables from rings left by drinks.

- If you see a kitchen or dining table that you'd really like for your living room, remember that you can cut the legs down to make it into a coffee table!

- Height is something to consider, and it is worth measuring the height of the sofa(s) or chairs surrounding the coffee table to make sure that it's not too high.

CLEARING OUT TABLE CLUTTER

Discard magazines every week or month depending on how often you receive them, and whether you've read them. If it's something you want to keep, remove it from the living room to a file or box – somewhere safe where it won't accidentally get thrown out with the recycling!

Televisions: Televisions are delicate things and require gentle cleaning to remove dust and fingerprints. Turn the TV off, and when it is cool wipe over the surface with a microfibre cloth. If the screen still looks dirty, invest in some special LCD wipes, designed for cleaning screens. Always check that what you are using is suitable for the type of television you have, as using the wrong type of product may damage it.

Speakers: Dust cloth-covered speakers using a duster, or use a very slightly dampened microfibre cloth to wipe down speakers without any covering.

Remote controls: We have so many different remote controls these days, it's hard to keep track of them all and their various uses. It can be useful to label them, saying what they're for, and find a specific place to keep them together.

Remote controls should be kept clean, something I admit to often forgetting to do myself. Use a duster or microfibre cloth to give them a gentle wipe down.

It's useful to keep a stock of spare batteries for all your various remotes: I find that the odds and ends drawer (see page 84) is a good and rather natural place for them to live.

FIREPLACES

We're lucky enough to have a proper fire, which I love. If you have an open fire, you should have your chimney swept about once a year – though it's worth saying that this is the general rule; how often you have your chimney swept will really depend on how often you use it, the type of fuel you use, and the type of chimney you have.

If you're only burning wood in your fire, take the fresh ash (once it's cold) and keep it in a sack in a dry place. Wait until the weather is dry, then scatter it around any fruit trees

you might have, or in your flowerbeds as a fertilizer and natural source of potassium. It is absorbed better in the growing season, so it might be wise to wait until spring.

We've still got a black metal fireback at the back of our fireplace, because we live in an old house, and we clean this with grate polish.

GAS FIRES

Gas fires are very good for a room that you don't use so often. When you have friends round, you can just flick on the fire and it will immediately bring a glow to the room; even if it's not very cold, you may find that it's a welcome thing.

They do need regular servicing. If you're having a new gas fire fitted and you think you are going to use it often, a remote control is brilliant; it's a terrific boon not to have to bend down and faff around with it.

MANTELPIECES

Whatever you keep on it – vases of flowers, picture frames, ornaments or candlesticks – the mantelpiece is one of the main focal points of the living room, so keep it tidy and dust it regularly.

THE HALLWAY

Shoes, wellingtons, umbrellas and coats always take
up more room than you think, so plan a special place
for them – often this will be by the front or back door,
but it depends on space, of course.

———————————

Garden shoes or boots can take up a
large area, but if you don't have this,
a basket or bench seat with a lid is useful
for shoes, boots, hats and gloves.

For jackets and coats, a coat stand is
ideal, but if you don't have room for
this, hooks on the wall or door are
a useful alternative. Coats can hang
at different levels: children's at the
bottom, adults' at the top.

Umbrellas stand up well in a tall barrel or bin.

This area is a good place to keep all
your **reusable totes and shopping
bags** too – otherwise it's very easy to
forget them on your way out.

Do have a clear-out every so often,
otherwise, especially in winter, things
can really pile up, and your coat stand
or similar can be burdened to the point
of toppling over!

If you have a **space under the stairs**, make the most of it! Fitted cupboards and drawers can
make this an ideal storage space.

SMOKE & CARBON MONOXIDE ALARMS

It is advisable to have one of each alarm on every floor of your home: make sure they are marked with a current British Standards or European (CE) safety mark.

If you are worried about the risk of fire in your home, book a free home fire safety visit.

Many models come with a low-battery warning, but make a note of the date when you put the batteries in and put a reminder in your diary to replace them in 12 months.

If you are worried you won't remember to replace the batteries every year, buy a 10-year alarm instead: you can't remove the batteries, and instead you should replace the whole alarm every 10 years.

Always test your alarms regularly to ensure that they are working. Make it part of your routine: do it at the same time as a household task that you do on a set day every week, like taking your recycling out.

RADIATORS

These are often forgotten, but do need cleaning. Start by vacuuming around, on top and underneath the radiator to get rid of any loose dust. If you have traditional column-style radiators, you can buy special flexible brushes for getting into the nooks and crannies – though a long-handled wooden spoon with a duster wrapped around the top will do the job too.

I find that radiators in busy areas tend to get marks on them – especially if you have bikes coming through the house. A cream cleaner, applied gently, should remove them.

THE HOME OFFICE

Lots of people work from home now, whether it's full or part time. If you fall into this category, you will know that you need your own space in which to work. If you can use a whole room, then of course that's ideal. I like having my office next to the kitchen, as I am always nipping in there for a cup of coffee or to get lunch on the go, and it is the centre of the house. However, this is a personal preference, and might not suit everyone: if your house is very noisy, it might make more sense for you to have your office further away from all the action and hubbub, where you can work undisturbed.

Often a big traditional desk with lots of drawers won't fit into the space you have available; maybe you use a ledge or a shelf, or have a bureau or a very small desk. Luckily computers and laptops are so portable now that you can get away with having less space to accommodate them. Make sure your room has plenty of plug sockets and a strong wi-fi connection.

If your work space is carved out of a room that serves another purpose – an open-plan kitchen, a living room, the bedroom, or even a hallway – it's important to make sure you have sufficient storage, whether that's cupboards, shelves, boxes, or A4 lever arch files in which to keep all your paperwork. You don't want invoices creeping on to your coffee table, or getting shoved in a kitchen drawer and then forgotten.

Whatever space you have available, it's well worth making the area pleasant. It's also very important that it's warm – if it's cold, I find that I don't feel much like working! If you're next to a draughty window, or if your office is outside in a shed (as I believe some people's are!), you might want to consider investing in a small electric heater. A large blanket or throw over your chair is a small but noticeable comfort, and for those who really feel the cold, a hot-water bottle is jolly nice too.

As with all areas of the house, lighting is terribly important. If you have a desk, a desk lamp is an obvious accessory. If you don't have room for a desk lamp, make sure the area is adequately lit, especially when it gets dark – this does happen within working hours in winter! It's important not to strain your eyes, so do make sure to take regular breaks from the screen too.

HOUSEHOLD ADMINISTRATION

───────────

'This sounds very grand, but you know what I mean.
Whether you work from home or not, you will inevitably
have paperwork and documents, some of them relating
to your home, that need to be kept safe.'

───────────

I'm not a trained secretary; my husband tells me that when you open a letter, you should deal with it straight away, but I'm very apt to open the whole post and just do something about the letter that I am particularly interested in and put everything else to one side. That's not how you should do it, though! Deal with post as you read it, rather than opening a letter, shoving it somewhere and then having to come back to it.

Some people find it useful to have a set time when they can go through paperwork. If you have bills to pay that don't come out of your account automatically, note down in your diary the details of when they need to be dealt with, so you don't forget. We increasingly receive less physical post than we used to, and much communication is done via email. The immediacy of the form and the fact that many people have access to their email on their smartphones means that senders often expect speedy responses. How you approach your email is up to you, and everyone will have their own opinion about what they think is appropriate, but it's certainly useful having some sort of system, and a rough deadline by which you are going to aim to reply, otherwise it is very easy for chaos to reign!

PERSONAL POSSESSIONS

KEYS & VALUABLES

It's best not to leave keys right by the door, where burglars can come in and just help themselves to them. Hang them on a hook on the back of a cupboard door, then you'll always know where they are. Label them with names like 'back door' and 'shed' (as it won't always just be you who's using them). If you have a letterbox opening in your door, make sure the keys aren't visible when you look through it.

If you keep a neighbour's spare set of keys, don't label them with the house name – if they are stolen, the burglar will go straight to 'Ivy Cottage' or whatever too! Label them by name – e.g. Lucy & Peter – so it's not too obvious.

Always have spare sets of important keys tucked away, and again, make sure that they're labelled. Some types of keys can be very expensive to replace, especially car keys, so look after them.

You may have a safe or a cupboard for important or valuable things, whether it's jewellery or deeds (you may keep the latter in the bank). Either way, make sure to keep everything together.

COMPUTER SCREENS, LAPTOPS, TABLETS & TOUCHSCREEN MOBILES

We own an increasing amount of technology, and considering how often we all touch our tablets or mobiles, it is worth taking the time to clean them properly and with care, as they are expensive. I pass the buck on to my grandchildren when they come to stay, because they know all about it: I just watch and say how clever they are.

- **Invest in a spray that is suitable for using on screens – they are designed to evaporate quickly without leaving streaks and are often made specifically for using on LCD and plasma screens. They can often be used to clean reading glasses too, so you can kill two birds with one stone.**

- **Turn your device off and make sure it's unplugged before beginning to clean it.**

- **Don't spray directly on to the screen and keyboard, but on to a cloth first. It should be moist rather than sopping wet. I am told by those who are more experienced in these matters that microfibre cloths are good for this task, as they don't leave lint that will show up on dark screens when they are turned off.**

Use an old toothbrush or cotton buds to help keep your keyboard clean and get rid of difficult to reach dust and dirt in between the keys. You can also buy cans of compressed air that are good for blasting out any stray crumbs . . .

DRYING OUT A PHONE IN RICE

Dropping or accidentally submerging your phone in water is a common modern-day malady. The most popular and often-repeated solution is to submerge the phone in dry rice for at least 24 hours, after turning it off. I've never tried this personally, but people do swear by it (though admittedly others have less luck). It is based on the practice of storing photographic film in silica (or, in a pinch, dried rice) to keep it dry when exposed to humid conditions. Whether or not the rice trick is effective, it's said that the best thing you can do for your phone when it's been exposed to wet or damp is to turn it off.

The experts say to wait until your computer or device is dry before turning it on again – which sounds sensible, although also a case of do as I say rather than as I do.

BOOKS & BOOKSHELVES

How you organize your books will all depend on how many books you have, how much space you have, and what your reading habits are. Everyone has their own favoured system, such as putting the authors alphabetically, which is certainly a great help when you want to find a particular novelist. I think the most useful thing you can do when it comes to organizing your shelves is to divide your books by genre and then put them in the places where you will need them. That way, if you only ever read in bed, you can make sure that there's a dedicated space in your room for the books you're keen to read. You might also want to keep travel books and maps together in the living room, text-books in the study, or dictionaries near where you play Scrabble! I have a great many cookery books and I tend to organize these by country and type, so that all the books on Chinese cookery are next to each other, and so on.

Lucy arranges novels into those she has read, and those she has still to read, which I think is very clever. I have friends who write their initials or their name in the front of books when they've read them, which is also handy for when you lend your books out, as it can be very easy for people to lose track of where they came from!

LAUNDRY & WARDROBE WISDOM

Grasp the nettle

'Grasping the nettle is very rewarding and something most of us, myself included, could do with when it comes to hand washing, ironing and clearing out wardrobes.'

I may be a dab hand at laundry now, but it wasn't always that way. When I was at Domestic Science College, as it was called then, we were taught how to do laundry by a marvellous and rather strict teacher called Miss Sutherland. I can remember having to wash and iron a man's V-neck sweater that I'd brought in from home. I obviously wasn't concentrating, as I put it on too hot a wash and when I took it out it had shrunk terribly. But I dried it and ironed it carefully anyway and when it came to being judged, the only comment from Miss Sutherland was, 'Well done, Mary, your child's sweater is beautifully presented.' I never said a word but I have been very careful about washing woollens ever since! Washing machines weren't common then, but I am very lucky – I've got a good washing machine now, and I set it on 30° for woollens as Miss Sutherland said and it works a treat.

'Grasp the nettle' is a phrase my husband often uses. It means don't faff about. In essence, stop talking about doing something and get on and do it. Grasping the nettle is very rewarding and something most of us, myself included, could do with when it comes to hand washing, ironing and clearing out wardrobes. But before you go grasp the nettle, learn from my experience and always pay attention to the instructions!

BEDS

PILLOWS

When I got married, I came with my own pillows – old spares from my parents. I never thought about them; the ends of the feathers would poke through, as you put the under-pillowcase on, and then you'd put the proper cover over the top and the little feathery ends of the feathers would still be there, pricking us. I didn't notice it for years and then we went to stay at the InterContinental Hotel on Park Lane during the Chelsea Flower Show, and the pillows were so comfortable. You've only got to go away to realize . . . After that, I went straight out and bought new, good-quality pillows – because once you've had amazing, soft down pillows, you realize that there are pillows and there are pillows, and unfortunately you do get what you pay for. They're terribly expensive, but as a special Christmas present to yourself, or someone else, they are a wonderful thing. If you've inherited your pillows, it's about time you had new ones! It's something our parents never did – you had a bed and pillows for life then – but we think differently now.

- There are many different types of pillow filling, ranging from synthetic fillings such as memory foam or microfibre to natural ones, such as feather, down or a mixture of the two. What you plump for is up to you, and will probably depend on how you sleep, and whether you have any allergies.

- Though they come in all sorts of shapes and sizes, the standard UK pillow measurement is 48cm x 74cm.

- Pillow protectors add an extra layer between your pillow and pillow cover (though they can sometimes make the latter a little tight). They protect your pillows from stains and are meant to prolong their life, though they aren't necessary.

- Pillows and duvets should be cleaned regularly (see page 158) and replaced reasonably often, especially if there are people with allergies in your family.

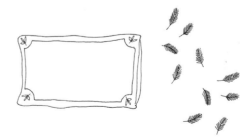

MATTRESSES

There are so many different options now, and what a good thing that is: you can get them soft on one side, hard on the other, orthopaedic (if you prefer a firmer texture), hypo-allergenic, made with natural fillings, made with memory foam . . . there really is a lot to choose from. But one thing is certain: if you're buying a new mattress, you should jolly well try it out first.

Remember that mattresses vary in depth, and that this will affect what type of fitted undersheet you need to buy, shallow or deep.

Mattress sizes (and, accordingly, duvet sizes) vary according to country – this is something that is worth bearing in mind if you're on holiday and tempted by bed linen on sale.

It is advisable – so the experts say! – to flip your mattress every few months, to get the most out of it, as it can become uneven over the years. Generally, a good mattress should last for at least 10 years – although, saying that, our first mattress made it to 40!

A mattress protector or padded topper is a very good idea (or both, if you want to be like the Princess and the Pea). They add an extra layer to your mattress, though they are slightly different:

• **Fitted mattress protectors do what they say – they protect your mattress from spills and stains, and help to keep sheets in position on the bed. They can be waterproof, padded, heated, or contain a filling that prevents dust mites, which can be helpful for allergy sufferers.**

- Mattress toppers are thicker, and more of an extension of your mattress, really, adding both height and comfort. They can be filled with duck feathers, wool, memory foam, or synthetic fibres.

BED LINEN

Fitted sheets are a huge joy, because they do stay on. I didn't realize until I visited a department store recently that some fitted sheets come in two depths: regular (up to 30cm) or deep fit (generally 32–36cm). Regardless of how thick your mattress is, a deep fit is easier to use. When storing fitted sheets, fold the corners in on each other before folding to create a tidy rectangle.

Pillowcases come in different styles and sizes but the two most common are the 'housewife' and the 'Oxford'. The main difference between them is that pillows fit snugly into housewife pillowcases, whereas Oxford pillowcases have an extra decorative detail of a 'flap' of fabric around the border of the pillow.

DUVETS

THESE ARE THE STANDARD UK SIZES FOR DUVETS AND MATTRESSES:

Single: W90cm x L190cm
Small double: W120cm x L190cm
Double: W135cm x L190cm
Kingsize: W150cm x L200cm
Super kingsize: W180cm x L200cm

How much insulation duvets offer – in other words, how warm they are – is measured in 'togs'. 15 is the highest, warmest rating. Duvets can be filled with natural feathers or synthetic fillings. What you choose is a matter of personal taste, but if you suffer from allergies, synthetic is probably a better option.

WASHING DUVETS & PILLOWS

Look out for dry-cleaning firms offering half-price duvet and pillow cleaning, and take advantage of any deals when you see them. You may be able to wash polyester pillows and duvets yourself (always read the label first, as brands and fillings vary greatly), though you may struggle to fit them into a domestic washing machine, depending on the size of the drum and load capacity.

Some people like crisp cotton sheets and duvet covers and are happy to iron everything: some people don't like ironing, and never bother. I like bed linen to be pristine-ish: I don't like a wrinkled look, but that's me, I'm old-fashioned.

If you don't want to iron, but don't want everything to look too crumpled, there are a few options:

- **Polycotton (i.e. half polyester and half cotton) bed linen doesn't require ironing, though it helps if you dry the sheets and covers flat. Because I like the feel of ironed pillowcases, I usually relent and end up ironing them.**

- **Textured cotton blend bed linen such as seersucker, which has a crimped look, dries nicely without requiring any additional elbow grease on your part.**

- **If you prefer natural fibres, and you aren't bothered about things being immaculate, it's possible to buy 'lazy linen' bedding styles that are designed to have a slightly crushed look.**

Thread count is something that is often mentioned when buying bedding. It refers to the number of horizontal and vertical threads woven together per inch (2.5cm) of fabric. The higher the thread count, the more luxurious it is meant to be. A thread count can be as high as 1,000, and it is priced accordingly.

There are many others you can choose between, including:

- **Brushed cotton:** has a cosy, flannel-like feel and is good for the colder months.

- **Jersey:** a light, stretchy fabric – rather like a t-shirt!

MAKING & CHANGING THE BED

Bed linen needs washing regularly, ideally once a week.
I suspect many people are not this fastidious, partly because
making the bed again is such a chore, but it is important!

HOSPITAL CORNERS

I can't say that the technique is something I've ever really thought about much, perhaps because I learnt how to make a bed with hospital corners at college. These days, fitted sheets are very popular and readily available, so you don't need to worry about a loose sheet if you don't want to. But if you do, here's how to do it:

1. Spread the top sheet over the mattress with the bottom width of the sheet tucked under.

2. Stand at one corner by the bottom of the mattress and pull up the edge of the sheet so it forms a triangle shape above the bed.

3. Tuck the part of the sheet hanging below the mattress underneath it.

4. Fold the sheet being held above the mattress over, flat against the edge of the mattress.

5. Tuck the overhanging part of the triangle underneath the mattress.

6. Treat the other three corners in the same way.

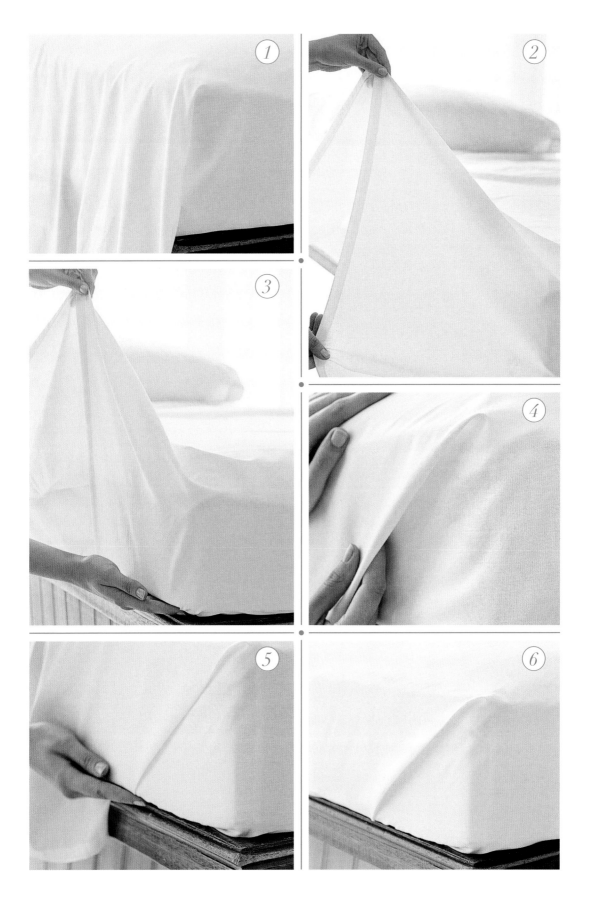

TIPS ON CHANGING THE DUVET

If you've got a duvet and you have difficulty in changing the cover – a lot of people hate changing the duvet cover, and I can't say I blame them – make life a little easier for yourself by putting a sheet under the duvet, then change all the sheets and pillowcases every fortnight, and just do the duvet cover once a month. Otherwise, try the techniques below:

CHANGING A DUVET WITH ANOTHER PERSON TO HELP

1. Lay the duvet cover out on the bed so that the opening is at the bottom.

2. Lay the duvet on top so that it is matched up to the case.

3. Each take one corner of the duvet and insert it into the opening, then shuffle it up to the correct corner.

4. Pinch the corners in place and shake the duvet out, easing the cover along it to the bottom.

5. Close the opening and arrange so it sits evenly.

CHANGING A DUVET COVER BY YOURSELF (SWISS ROLL METHOD)

1. Turn the duvet cover inside out and lay it out flat on the bed so that the opening is at the top (the pillow end).

2. Place the duvet on top of the cover so that it's all matched up and the corners are aligned.

3. Starting from the end of the bed, roll the duvet and cover in on themselves like you're making a Swiss roll.

4. When you get to the top of the bed, push the duvet-roll into one corner of the duvet cover, turning it the right way out as you do so.

5. Repeat with the other corner, then unfurl the middle as well.

6. Unroll the duvet back up to the end of the bed and give it a little shake, then close the opening, flip it the right way round and arrange so it sits evenly.

KEEPING COSY

I tend to feel the cold, so electric blankets and hot-water bottles are of prime importance to me. As with most things to do with beds, whether you opt for these is a matter of personal preference: some people may prefer a cooler bed. That said, you can buy electric blankets and duvets that are heated half and half and have dual controls. I had one of these when my husband and I were first married, and I discovered that it was actually on the wrong way round, and my husband had been too polite to say that I kept cooking him! If you do have an electric blanket or duvet, always carefully read and follow the instructions about leaving it on.

Quilts and blankets folded across the end of the bed can look very nice, if you like that kind of thing; not only do they add extra warmth, but they conceal a slightly rumpled duvet.

WASHING, DRYING & IRONING CLOTHES

WASHING MACHINES

A washing machine is a big outlay, and which one you choose will depend on your budget. It is well worth looking on Which? (which.co.uk) when you want to buy something like this, because they are unbiased and non-profit-making and do the time-consuming research for you. Common variants to consider are: load size, spin speed, energy rating, noise level – and, of course, price.

My machine was rather expensive compared with many others, but you get what you pay for, and I've had mine for many years now. You can buy much cheaper ones, but they may not last as long.

- **Washer-dryers are a good solution for people in small households who don't have a high turnover of washing – or enough space for both a washing machine and a tumble dryer.**

- **When choosing a washing machine, remember to measure the space where you're intending it to go – and make sure that there is sufficient room for the door of the machine to open fully!**

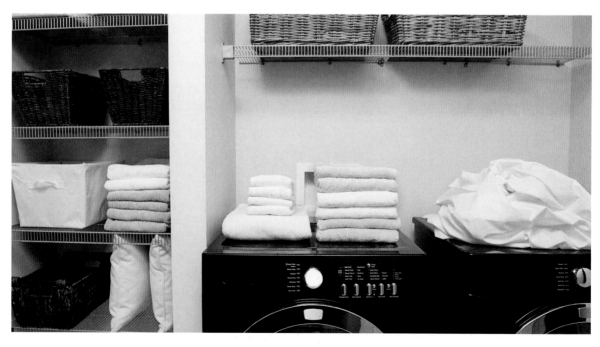

TIPS ON HOW TO USE YOUR WASHING MACHINE EFFICIENTLY

Don't overload it; there should be a 10cm gap at the top of the drum, so don't be tempted to cram it full.

Remove the detergent drawer every few months and wash it with warm soapy water to remove any build-up.

Wash bras with an underwire in mesh bags – not only does this protect them, but it stops the wire getting stuck in your machine if it comes out.

Remove the filter: first place a towel on the floor and have a large bowl ready to collect any water that comes out. Take out the filter, get rid of any debris it's collected and brush out with an old toothbrush. Give the filter a good soak before replacing (the filter is normally located at the bottom of the machine, but check the manual if you can't find it – the manual will also tell you how often you should clean it).

Check pockets (or encourage your family to!) for loose change or hairclips – and rogue tissues – which can get caught in the drum.

Run an empty cycle to clear the machine drum, and add a cut lemon to a short empty cycle to keep the machine fresh.

WASHING CLOTHES

- To carry dirty clothes from the laundry basket to the washing machine, lay the largest item (e.g. a shirt) on the bed, then pile the rest in the centre. Bring up the corners and make them into a bundle you can carry – this prevents you dropping socks and pants along the way!

- Always separate your washing into dark colours, similar-toned bright colours and whites. No matter how colour-fast you think something might be, it's not worth the risk. It's obvious but worth repeating.

- If you want to test the colour-fastness of a garment – a new pair of jeans, say – wet a little patch of the fabric and rub it on a clean white tea towel to see if any dye comes off.

- Turn trousers and jeans inside out before washing – this prevents them collecting fluff and also seems to make their colour last longer.

- Follow the labels on clothes: that's what they're there for, and aren't we lucky to have them.

- The slight exception to the above is when the label says 'dry clean only'. Remember that the manufacturers are only covering themselves so that if you wash the garment, you are doing so at your own risk. If you want to, why not be brave and have a go? I often wash so-called precious fabrics with great success.

- Washing powder or liquid – what you use is really up to you. Everybody's got their favourite: maybe it's what your mother had, or what you yourself like the smell of, or find cares well for your clothes. They're all much of a muchness, I think.

- Quick washes are convenient for when you're in a rush, but generally suited to lightly dirty items.

One of the biggest disasters when washing is a forgotten tissue in a pocket – you just know it'll go all over that black skirt and you'll have to take a lint roller to it – so it's worth trying to remember to check for strays before you put a load on. Tissues in pockets should be banned!

STAINS

Stains are always best treated fresh, if possible: speed is the essence of success when it comes to shifting them. It's also important not to panic and start scrubbing away. The first thing to do is to gently dab at the affected area with a dry cloth or kitchen paper to remove the worst of it, or, if it's a solid stain, scrape it off as cleanly as possible with something like a blunt knife. Only once you've done that should you think about the stain that is left behind.

There are a few key rules to remember:

- **Remove the excess before you treat the stain.**

- **Blot or dab. Scrubbing or squeezing can embed the stain into the fabric.**

- **Use a white cloth or kitchen paper rather than something coloured.**

- **Use cool water to ensure that the stain doesn't dry out before treatment.**

- **If using a stain removal product, read the instructions and test it on an inconspicuous area first to check that the garment is colour-fast.**

- **Once you've removed the worst of it, soak first, then wash as normal.**

Most modern stain removers are designed to treat a spectrum of stains, from protein-based liquids (e.g. blood), to oil and grease, drinks containing tannins, and cosmetics. It's worth stocking up on a selection so you have all bases covered, and making sure you buy a product suitable for use on delicates like silk and woollens.

I'm a great one for pre-soaking before washing, and I always soak whites and other colours separately, with a different laundry powder for each. If you do this, you don't have to scrub them or do anything else to them. Scrubbing collars and other areas that tend to mark does wear out the fabric – soaking is more gentle on the garments. It works for me.

Always soak in cool water: if the water is too hot it can set the stain.

COMMON STAINS

Red wine is one of the most dreaded of all stains – especially when it spills on something light coloured. It will come out with the right products, so it's wise to have these in the cupboard. Table salt helps to soak up the wine and is something that most of us always have to hand; cover the affected area immediately and then press against it gently with a cloth – the salt crystals should soak up the excess liquid.

Candle wax is something that often drips on to tablecloths and sleeves: Scrape away as much hardened wax as you can then cover the affected area with greaseproof paper and iron on a low setting – the heat should melt any remaining wax, which should then be absorbed by the paper. If the wax was coloured and has left a mark, wash the item with an appropriate stain removal product.

Lily stamens: Dab the affected area immediately with a piece of sticky tape to remove the loose pollen.

Make-up around collars and necklines: Wipe with make-up remover wipes or baby wipes as soon as you notice the stain, then soak with biological laundry powder before washing as usual.

WASHING, DRYING & IRONING SYMBOLS

	Hand wash only
40°	Cottons wash
40°	Synthetics wash
30°	Wool wash
	Not suitable for washing
	Suitable for tumble drying
	Tumble dry at lower temperature
	Tumble dry at higher temperature
	Do not tumble dry
	Suitable for dry cleaning
	Do not dry clean
	Cool iron
	Warm iron
	Hot iron
	Do not iron

DELICATES & WOOLLENS

If you've an old washing machine that hasn't got a special Delicates or Wool setting, don't use it for these items – it's a risky business, and you don't want to find out that your machine isn't up to it the hard way, by ruining a favourite blouse. Instead, wash garments by hand in a clean sink or tub, then dry them flat.

Some people spin their delicates and woollens on the gentlest setting and for a short period (no more than 5 minutes), but I have a special method for helping wool and cashmere jumpers and cardigans to dry. It's particularly useful if you have to hand wash these items, as it can be very difficult to remove water gently, and you don't want everything dripping on to your floor or taking days to air dry and be smelling damp.

1. After you have taken out as much water as you can from the item (either by hand, gently, or by spinning slowly for no more than 5 minutes), lay it on a towel and spread it out in a beautiful shape.

2. Cover your garment with another towel, roll it all up, then stamp on it! This helps the extra water to come out. Lay it out flat to finish drying – it shouldn't take any time at all after this.

3. Once they have served their purpose, post-stamping, this is a good opportunity to pop your towels into the wash.

WASHING TOWELS

Towels and bath mats need to be washed every week. If you have hard water, a dryer will help to make them fluffy again, and you can also use a fabric softener – otherwise they can dry as stiff as boards. Too much fabric softener can reduce how absorbent they are, though, so be sparing.

HOW TO HAND WASH DELICATE ITEMS

1. Fill a tub with cool water and the recommended quantity of a delicate fabric detergent (not regular granules).

2. Add garments of a similar colour (but don't overfill).

3. Leave to soak for at least 15 minutes before massaging them to help clean.

4. Leave to soak again for another 5–10 minutes – depending how dirty the items are.

5. Drain and rinse, filling the tub with clean water – make sure it is clear and there's no residual detergent.

6. Leave to soak, then drain and either put into your machine on a gentle spin or place between towels as per my method on page 172!

AIR DRYING

- If you are drying washing outside, make sure your washing line and pegs are both clean, or you could undo all the work you've just done!

- Clothes drying racks come in all shapes and sizes now, and many have sections that extend outwards, for laying down garments that need to be dried flat. Tall and thin dryers will save on floor space when in use, and most drying racks can be folded neatly away to save on storage space. Little dryers that can be hung over radiators are also useful, especially in the cooler months of the year. You can also buy electrically heated racks that gently evaporate moisture for speedier drying times.

- Taking the time to smooth out creases in clothes and hanging them to dry with care can cut down on ironing – or at least reduce creases. Shirts can be dried very nicely on a plastic hanger, buttoned up and seams smoothed and aligned.

IRONING

If you are the ironing sort, or if you wear a crisp white or silk shirt every day (which makes you the ironing sort by default), what an innovation the modern steam iron is for you, going a great way towards taking the agony out of the process. Generally the more steam your iron produces, the more quickly it will remove creases and wrinkles from fabrics.

Regular steam irons have a container of water and a steam function and are fairly portable.

Steam generator irons sit on a separate water-filled base (so they are fairly bulky) and create more steam than conventional irons, getting the job done more quickly. Well worth it if you have a regular mountain of ironing each week, as they do the job amazingly well and give a very good finish, but they are frightfully expensive.

IRONING TIPS

- A too-hot iron will ruin your clothes, so always read the garment care label before you start! See page 171 for a guide to the symbols.

- Before you begin it can be useful to separate your ironing into piles according to fabric (cotton, synthetics, knitwear and so on) – this way you can keep your iron on the relevant temperature setting until you move on to the next fabric type.

- It's worth investing in a good thick cover (or special padding that sits between the board and cover) for your ironing board: it will make the process of ironing easier, and decrease the likelihood of metal mesh patterns appearing on clothes.

- Some clothes should be turned inside out before ironing, as a protective measure to stop the fabric becoming singed or shiny. Generally dark colours benefit from being ironed inside out, and jeans are easier to manage too.

- Some fabrics are better ironed slightly damp: linen and silk both fall into this category.

- Cover delicate garments with a protective cotton cloth while ironing – an old tea towel or napkin will do. This also protects against watermarks on silks and chiffons.

- Allow your iron to stand for a few minutes between temperature changes to be sure it has adjusted.

- In hard water areas, always use distilled water in steam irons.

IRONING SHIRTS

If chaps or chapesses are working in a formal environment and they need to wear shirts, it's expensive to send them to a laundry. To make this chore less arduous, I find the method below most efficient for speedy ironing. It also ensures that you are not causing more creases as you go along.

1. When I iron a shirt, I start off by doing the collar, then the cuffs and sleeves, as they don't crease as easily as the body.

2. Next, I place the shoulder of the shirt on to the thinnest part of the ironing board, and remove all creases, before repeating on the other side.

3. Then I do one side of the body, and gradually shuffle the shirt away from me, ironing as I go, until I've reached the other side.

4. Finally, I run the iron across the collar again, do up the top button, and put it on a hanger.

HOW TO FOLD A SHIRT

If you need to fold rather than hang your shirts or blouses, either to put on a shelf or into a suitcase, make sure that you don't undo the hard work you put into the ironing.

1. First button the shirt (do up all the buttons as this will help to minimize creases).

2. Lay it buttoned-side down on a flat surface, making sure it's nice and smooth.

3. Hold up one sleeve and fold down a small section of the corresponding side of the shirt.

4. Fold the sleeve in on itself. Repeat with the other sleeve.

5. Fold the bottom third of the shirt into the middle.

6. Fold the top section of the shirt on top of that and smooth down.

STORING & CARING FOR CLOTHES AND SHOES

STORING CLOTHES

In an ideal world you might separate winter clothes from summer clothes, arrange everything by both colour and type, so have all your navy things together, then all your scarves together and so on. It's all a matter of what space you've got, though. Many people keep their shoes in shoe boxes, but I find that takes up too much room.

- If you like, you can line old drawers with lining paper or even a spare roll of wallpaper.

- Store precious or light-coloured things that are likely to get dust on them in zipped polythene bags (this will also protect them from moths, see pages 188–9). For dresses, skirts, jackets and coats, you can use a dry-cleaner's see-through bag, or zippered protective bags. I put things I don't use very often – swimwear, holiday clothes, thermal vests and winter scarves – in separate polythene boxes.

CLEARING OUT CLOTHES

Every so often, I will sort through the chaos that is my wardrobe. I don't enjoy it much, but it's wonderful once it's done.

I don't think I'm a hoarder, but I don't like throwing things away! Sometimes you really do have to be ruthless and have a good clear-out, though, especially if you are tight on space.

When I run out of room in the wardrobe, I go through my clothes and shoes and sort them into three piles: items to be passed on to friends or family (warm jumpers often go to my daughter, who lives quite an outdoor life), items to go to charity shops, and things that have come to the end of their life and need to be chucked away.

- Many charities provide details online of items that they accept and don't accept – and things that they particularly need. These can vary greatly depending on the charity: some shops take furniture, for example, so it is worth doing some research before you start sorting out your things.

- When you are giving clothes to your local charity shop or clothes bank, do make sure that they are clean – give them in the condition you would like to receive them.

- There are some items of clothing that you might never wear again but can't bear to part with, either for sentimental reasons, or because they are too special to give away. If you have the room, you can put these in protective zippered clothes bags (to protect them from moths and dust) and store them somewhere else: I have another wardrobe I use for this purpose. This way they won't take up prime space in your own wardrobe, where it makes much more sense to prioritize the things you do wear. You can pack them into a box with a lid or an old chest and store them in a loft or attic if you have room, but keep them well away from damp and pests.

LOOKING AFTER SHOES

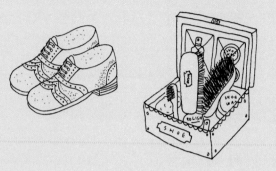

When it comes to shoes, I tend to go for comfort every time, with a few heels for special occasions. It really is worth having good shoes soled and heeled – it's expensive now, but it does prolong their life. Keep an eye on your heels, and don't let them get worn down too far, as this can make your trip to the cobblers even more costly.

Most of my shoes are black and brown, as my husband is brilliant at cleaning them – that's his Army training – but he doesn't do coloured shoes.

Keep all shoe cleaning items together in a box or tin – it makes sense to keep this near where you might clean your shoes.

Some people have rules about taking off shoes at home. In our house, we're not that fussy, but we do scrub them and see that they're dry before wandering through the house. For this reason, we make sure that we have large doormats by the door.

STORING SHOES

I built shelves into my cupboard that are exactly the length of my shoes and I just store them all the way along this, with all the black shoes together and so on (though it doesn't always stay this way). Underneath is a taller shelf for boots. I find this an efficient way of using space, and it's easy to see what's there at a glance – sometimes when shoes are put back into boxes, you can forget what's inside, and that's assuming that they have been put back into their correct boxes! If you would like to build shelves like this, really the most important thing is to remember to measure your shoes – your highest pair of boots, and your longest pair of shoes (though your shoes may all be a similar size, things like pointed toes can add to their length) – to ensure that everything fits. Alternatively have a box or basket for your shoes at the bottom of your wardrobe.

*Use cotton dust bags, if your shoes came with them –
especially for pairs with embellished detailing where dust
can get trapped and be hard to shift.*

CARING FOR SHOES

If you get caught in the rain and come in and your shoes are damp, it's well worth shoving crumpled newspaper into them once you've taken them off: this helps to rebuild the shape of the shoe as they dry. Don't be tempted to put them on the radiator or too close to the Aga – it's better to let them dry out slowly, I find.

SUEDE

Whether it's winter boots, a sheepskin jacket or a handbag, suede should always be sealed with protective spray. Usually, the shop where you buy your suede item will also sell a spray (and will suggest that you buy it), but check you haven't got some at home already; I've got about five in the cupboard because I never remember! Spray your suede item as soon as you get home – preferably do this outside, if it's dry, as it can be rather strong-smelling stuff and has a tendency to linger. If you put your new suede item away in the cupboard, you're sure not to be able to remember if you've sprayed it or not.

It's well worth spraying anything suede twice, giving it a double layer of protection. Also, remember that you do have to repeat this process: the spray doesn't last for ever. If you wear your suede boots a few times a week, you will need to spray them more frequently, brushing them first with a suede brush, to ensure they remain protected from rain and other spills. Read the instructions on the back of the product carefully: they will tell you how often you should apply it.

All you need to brush off any dry dirt is a suede brush – the thicker the bristle, the more gentle you should be when wielding it.

REVIVING SUEDE

Even if you think nothing of a red wine spill on a pale shirt, the thought of cleaning suede can be a bit daunting.

I have found a very good method for reviving suede, especially when it has been squashed down and gone a bit flat or shiny through wear:

1. Half fill a kettle and put it on to boil (on the hob, if you have a suitable kettle).

2. When the steam starts coming out of the spout, hold up the suede, so that the steam is directed on to the marked area – be careful when doing this, as it is very easy to burn yourself on the steam, as I have discovered . . . (if you do catch your hand, stick it in a bowl of cold water immediately, and keep it there as long as you can – see page 57).

3. Repeat until you have steamed all the affected areas, and they look darker.

4. Use a towel or piece of kitchen paper to blot the excess moisture.

5. Brush immediately with a suede brush; like magic, the pile will be brought up.

VELVET

Velvet is a luxurious fabric and popular in winter for all those Christmas parties. Caring for it is very similar to caring for suede: use a textile protector spray suitable for velvet, and brush off any dry dirt with a soft shoe brush. Velvet that has turned a bit dull can be restored using the steaming method for suede described on page 185.

LEATHER

Leather shoes and boots need polishing to keep them supple.

It really is worthwhile cleaning coloured shoes with the appropriate colour polish, if you can find it, to cover up the scuffs. If your shoes are a natural colour in perfect condition (lucky you), you can use a clear polish.

If you have leather boots or shoes that get more than ordinary use – perhaps you wear them several times a week or for country walks – it's worth waterproofing them with a sealant. Like suede spray, this is something that should be applied as soon as you get your new shoes home, and that may also need to be reapplied periodically, to ensure that the shoes continue to be resistant to water.

SILK AND SATIN

These fabrics tend to be very delicate and should always be treated with a suitable textile protector spray. Check the weather forecast before you wear them: forewarned is forearmed! If the worst happens, many shoe companies will be happy to advise you on how to repair damage to their products. It's also well worth finding a cobbler you trust.

FABRIC & TRAINERS

Check the label of your trainers first to see if they can be washed in the machine. I pre-treat any dirty marks then put them into the machine to wash, as with everything else, at 30°C. I always try to put a few other things in there too, otherwise they can make a hell of a racket tumbling around. Nothing delicate, of course – old towels are perfect.

As soon as they're done, take them out and either put shoe trees into them or stuff them with newspaper to build the shape of the trainer up again. Leave them in a warm place to dry naturally, but don't put them anywhere very hot, or next to direct heat, like by a radiator.

RUBBER & WELLINGTONS

Clean wellingtons off with a hose, or under the tap, after using them, otherwise, next time you pull them on, you might be getting in somebody else's car and taking your boots and all their attached dried mud with you, which will leave a real mess. I notice some people have special bags for carrying wellingtons in; I just have a super-market bag, and it does me fine!

REPAIRING CLOTHES

MOTHS

Moths are the bane of my life, as we live in an old house, but we go on. They lay their eggs in spring, leaving a little white strip behind when they do so, and thrive in warm, dark conditions, meaning that the less cold the winter, the greater the potential for damage to the items you have packed away. Moths are discerning creatures: they love natural fibres, including silk and cotton, but are particularly partial to softer and finer fibres, such as wool and, the most luxurious of all, cashmere.

There are all sorts of moth-proofing products, chemical and natural – adding chestnuts or lavender sachets to your sock drawer and so on. But these tend not to be effective – they're meant to put moths off, but in my opinion, you don't want them to be there at all! Of course, use whatever pleases you, though: the scent of lavender bags is very nice.

Whether your home has moths – as many do – or not, these are the steps you need to take to preserve your best knitwear:

- **Clean your clothes: especially winter clothes and knitwear that you put away. Moths prefer clothes that are a little bit dirty. Be sure to repair any holes before cleaning moth-damaged items, as washing can make them worse – see page 189.**

- **Store clean woollies in resealable, zip-lock polythene bags. You can find these in supermarkets or online, and they will keep your clothes absolutely safe, if you make sure to keep them sealed.**

Once you've got moths, it's very difficult to get rid of them:
they can come under doors and through gaps in the floorboards . . .

- Perhaps you've noticed a tiny little hole in the shoulder of a jumper, as recently happened to me. First of all, mend it, then take all your jumpers, making sure they are clean, put them into sealed polythene bags and put them into the freezer for 24 hours – this will kill off

the moths' eggs. If you have a small freezer and have to do this in batches, then do. It's awfully boring, but it's the only way to really be sure that you've got rid of them. If your freezer is a little tight on space, you might want to turn to page 22 for tips on defrosting it.

MORE ON MOTHS

If you have carpets or rugs you must be especially vigilant: as long as you vacuum your carpets thoroughly and regularly, using a small nozzle to get into all the corners, and moving any furniture that needs moving, you won't get moths in carpets.

Vacuum your curtains too and, if they are made from a natural fibre, have them dry cleaned if you need to. Do check the label or care instructions that came with them, though, as washing can run the risk of causing them to shrink, especially if they are lined. Net curtains and any that are made of man-made fibres should be fine to wash, but again, always check the care instructions before doing so.

FIXING HOLES

No matter how much care you take of your things, holes, snags, tears and pulls do happen – and you just know they will happen to your favourite cardigan. When they do, don't despair: repair!

Don't wash the item, as this could cause the hole to become larger, making it more difficult to repair. If you think the hole is caused by a moth, you can wash the item after you have repaired it.

Use a thread that is as close in colour as possible to the item you're repairing – that way, even if you don't have the finest needlework, it won't be as visible.

Don't pull the stitches too hard when sewing up the hole, otherwise you risk putting too much strain on the fibres and you may soon end up with another hole.

If in doubt, consult someone who does invisible mending. They are specialists and really can work wonders.

WORN & BOBBLY WOOLLENS

I have a tortoiseshell style comb with metal teeth that I use for combing across pilled jumpers. They usually come in a couple of sizes, and it's best to buy the big one, because it covers a greater area, meaning you do less work. You can usually find them in supermarkets, department stores or haberdasheries.

Battery operated de-bobbling or clothes shaver machines are fairly inexpensive and are very useful for giving new life to pilled knitwear and wool jackets and coats – though they should be used with caution on fine fabrics such as cashmere (machines vary, so read the instructions carefully to see what is recommended).

If you wear a lot of dark colours, or have pets, a lint roller is a wardrobe wonder: it takes seconds to roll the sticky surface over garments to pick up hair, lint and dust – and even the white fluff that comes from leaving a tissue in a pocket in the washing machine (see page 167). If you have upholstered furniture, it's good for that too.

You can buy stone 'pilling removers': pumice-like, natural stones designed to be gently rubbed across garments with pilling and fluffy balls, effectively removing them. They come highly recommended and can be ordered online.

JEWELLERY

CLEANING JEWELLERY

I don't wear precious jewellery much, but most people have the odd ring, and if you want it to sparkle, it ought to be clean: it's surprising how mucky they can get, so you should give them a clean from time to time (see below).

When I got engaged, my mother said to me, 'You're far more likely to lose your engagement ring by leaving it on the side of a washbasin than by having it stolen,' and on the whole it does seem safest to keep it on all the time, particularly in public places, where it would be so easy for somebody to pick it up. If you are at home, and washing a load of heavy pans by hand, it might be worth removing any rings with precious stones, as it's very easy to knock them, and if you do this at the wrong angle, it can cause a fissure. Do always make sure to keep them in a safe place where you will remember them, though – or if you wear a necklace, you could thread them on to that.

I use an old soft nailbrush – you could also use a soft toothbrush – and a little pot or mug of warm soapy water: if I'm in the kitchen, I use washing-up liquid, and if I'm in the bathroom,

I might use a bit of shampoo. I brush both sides of the ring gently, give it a rinse and dry it carefully.

Gold chains can also be washed in soapy water. Pearls can be wiped gently with a clean damp cloth.

STORING JEWELLERY

You can buy special divider boxes with lots of little pockets for your jewellery that are made to go inside drawers, which is a very good idea for keeping things tidy, easy to find and untangled.

Another very good way to store non-precious jewellery is to insert a row of hooks inside a cupboard door, and hang your necklaces from them. I try to keep my colours separate, which makes everything very easy to find. It's not a good idea to heap necklaces on top of each other, because they'll scratch each other and get entwined, and you'll waste a lot of time trying to unravel them from each other – which can be a frustrating and time-consuming task.

Earrings are best kept in their pairs (if they come in pairs – some don't now!), in little boxes or a large box with dividers.

PACKING

Everyone has their own methods (I have a friend who packs things beautifully, with layers of tissue paper in between her folded dresses and so on, which is lovely but not practical for everyone), but some things are common sense.

PACKING TIPS

- Go for a light, strong suitcase, because it will be heavy enough by the time you've added everything. A suitcase on wheels is an enormous help, because nowadays you have to walk for miles at airports.

- Depending on your needs and how often you travel, it can be useful to have a couple of sizes of suitcase: one larger one, and one that is small enough to be taken on board as hand luggage. It's worth researching different airlines' policies regarding the size and weight of both hand luggage and checked luggage, as these can vary considerably, and also change frequently. It is also worth having a pair of digital bathroom or luggage scales, if you don't already, so that you can weigh your luggage and make sure you're not over the limit. Some airlines allow you to take a handbag in addition to your hand luggage; others don't and are very strict about it.

- Always check the weather forecast! You don't want to carry lots of jumpers and cardigans if it's going to be warm, but nor do you want to be caught out.

- My husband has a packing list for when he goes away, which is a very good idea. Next time you go somewhere with a hot climate, jot down what you wore when you get back. Keep it in your diary or somewhere safe, because you'll be going away in another year, and the fact that you can remember that you wore such and such clothes (and remembered to take a cardigan because of cold evenings) should save you the time of deciding what to pack again.

- Similarly, keep all the things you only really need when you go on holiday, like adaptors, and spare chargers, and mosquito repellent, all in one bag, so you don't have to scrabble around looking for all the individual items at the last minute. (But remember that mosquito and insect repellent can go off!)

- Keep valuable items, travel documents, and money in your hand luggage.

- If you are locking your checked luggage, it's worth noting that many airlines advise you to use a TSA approved lock. Security rules may require that your suitcase be opened to be inspected: TSA approved locks can be unlocked and relocked by airport security, but in some countries, such as the US, if you have another type of lock or strap you run the risk of your suitcase being forcibly opened, which may result in it being damaged.

- Put heavy things at the bottom of the suitcase – that is, the bottom of the suitcase when it is upright.

- Packing well is really about making the best use of the space you have; instead of taking shoe trees, roll up underwear, tights and socks and keep them in your shoes – this will help them to keep their shape in addition to being an efficient use of space.

- If you're taking creams and lotions and things like that, it's a good idea to put them into individual zipper poly bags before putting them in a toiletry bag, because you don't want any spillages. If you want to be really safe, put your toiletry bag in a poly bag (or reuse an old plastic bag) too.

- If you are taking something that's fragile, wrap it in plastic bags, bubble wrap or tissue paper and surround it with a layer of woolly jumpers on top and bottom, so that it is protected. While there is no failsafe way to guarantee the safety of your item, this will at least minimize the chance of it breaking.

- Write your name, address, telephone number and email on a piece of paper or a label and put it inside your suitcase where it's easily visible. I'm told you shouldn't advertise it on the outside, but if your suitcase gets lost, you want to maximize the chance of it being returned to you.

- Personalize your suitcase by tying coloured ribbons to its handle so you can recognize it easily. It's amazing how many black suitcases there are and how similar they all look.

- It is always advisable to invest in travel insurance. It can sometimes be added to house insurance at a good price. Always read the small print!

- The real secret to packing, I find, is to do it two days ahead, and let everything sink down in your suitcase. It's amazing how this happens: you shut it up, and down it goes. You do get some creases, but you also get it all in . . .

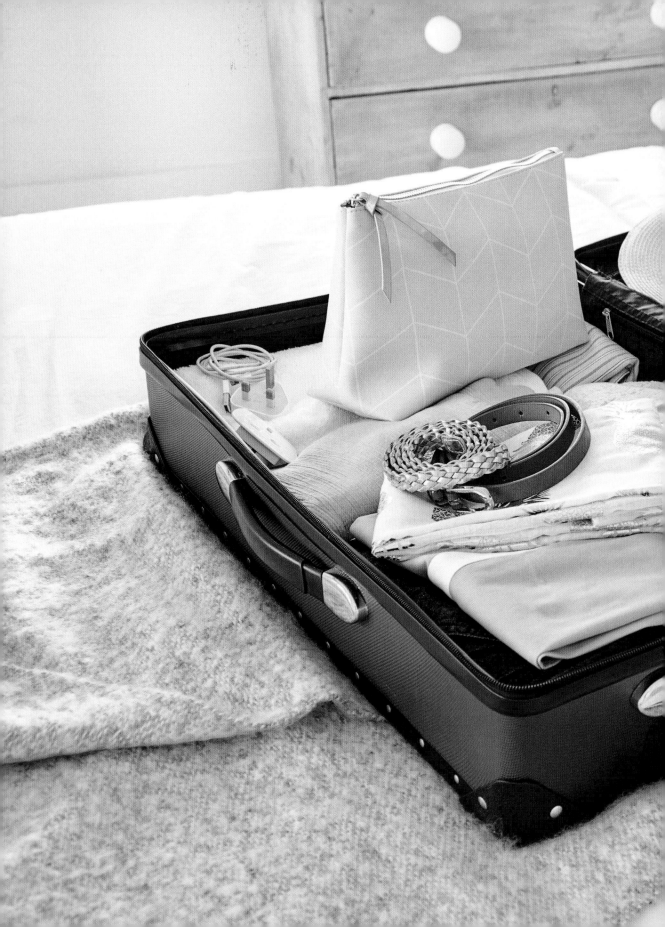

GARDENING & FLOWERS

Green fingers

'Whether you have a small garden, a yard, a little window box or two acres, growing things can be enormously rewarding.'

GARDENING

There is so much to say about gardens that it would be impossible for me to cover everything in one chapter, but I hope that what follows will encourage beginners to get going, and also show you that you don't need a garden to bring plants into your home. When I was growing up, my parents had a garden, and I remember helping my dad with picking raspberries and strawberries! Gardening was always something that was in the back of my mind, but it wasn't until I had a bit more time, and my children had started to grow up properly and needed less of my attention, that it really became a passion of mine.

Of course, it's great to garden with children too, and schools are now teaching it, which is a wonderful thing; the Royal Horticultural

Society (RHS) are promoting it as well. Children love to be given a little patch of garden, but you've got to do it with them, that's how they learn, and you should choose things that grow quickly, like lettuces, radishes and carrots. My grandson, Hobie, has a little garden and he does the lettuces, herbs and tomatoes. He waters them and picks them, and so on, and it's a wonderful thing.

Size notwithstanding, the type of garden you have will vary according to whether you are single, a couple or have children. Whatever type you have, though, as a rule it's good to grow what you enjoy, and if you have an area where you are able to pick things, how lovely. If you don't have room for vegetables, salads or herbs, you could grow these in gaps in between flowers.

Plants need looking after, and a garden can be a huge job – but there are gardens and then there are *gardens*. I started my married life with a small back yard, but no one could have been busier gardening than me. I'd tell friends that I couldn't possibly go away for the weekend, because I was too busy doing my pots! Now that we have a much bigger garden, I've realized how I was making a mountain out of a molehill, but I did start growing all sorts of things in my beloved pots. Whether you have a small garden, a yard, a little window box or two acres, growing things can be enormously rewarding.

What varieties of plants will do well in your outside space all depends on where you live, your soil, how mild it is, and also how sheltered. Some people in sheltered places

can have ordinary little cyclamen that you can buy in a supermarket all through the winter; we certainly couldn't, because it's too cold and they'd get frost damage. Start by looking round garden centres: see what's growing and looking good there, and read some books on how to plant (see page 207 for my recommendations). It's always helpful to see what works for your neighbour, too. You will soon learn what grows well.

If you get the bug, there are very good lectures and talks which can be great fun to go to, either at garden centres or at various RHS centres throughout the country. I've been a member of the RHS for over 30 years and am now an ambassador, and I find them to be an invaluable source of advice.

Take inspiration from what's around you and take note of other people's gardens.

THE NATIONAL GARDEN SCHEME OPENS UP GARDENS FOR CHARITY AND LISTS ONLINE ALL THE GARDENS THAT ARE OPEN AND THE DATES THAT YOU CAN SEE THEM: SEARCH BY YOUR POSTCODE TO FIND THE ONES NEAR YOU, AND GO AND LOOK AT THEM. USE THESE VISITS TO GET IDEAS: YOU CAN SEE WHAT GROWS WELL IN YOUR AREA, SOMETIMES YOU CAN BUY PLANTS – AND YOU MIGHT GET A GOOD TEA AS WELL! IT'S A GREAT DAY OUT AND IT'S NOT EXPENSIVE.

ALLOTMENTS

For keen gardeners without access to outdoor space, an allotment can be a wonderful thing. Not only can you grow your own fruit and veg, but tending an allotment is a fun and wholesome weekend and holiday activity for all the family – children can help with picking and sowing (and eating the spoils). Community gardens are a wonderful way to meet people in your local area and to share skills, ideas and the produce too. Waiting list times vary according to where you live and some councils can be very oversubscribed, but it is worth registering. You can find out more about your options and applying here: www.gov.uk/apply-allotment.

POTS &
HANGING BASKETS

For pots, evergreens are always a good option. As their name suggests, they last all the year round (bay trees and box bushes are two good examples). It can also be nice to change your pots with the seasons: in summer, annuals such as geraniums, petunias, nemesias and trailing plants, and heathers, cyclamen or pansies in autumn and winter.

Hanging baskets and pots need to be watered regularly, otherwise they don't absorb the water. When we lived in London and didn't have much outside space, we had a hanging basket outside the front door (a sunny spot that was lovely) and I would water it when I put the empty milk bottles out, filling one of the bottles with water so the basket was always slightly damp – not only was it killing two birds with one stone, but it was a good way of remembering to do the watering, too! Even if you don't have milk deliveries, you still need a routine.

Change the soil in your pots once a year, and remember that the compost should be slightly below the top of the pot, and not level with it – you want the soil to hold the water, not for the water to run off.

Just like animals (and humans!), plants need to be fed. I tend to use plant food that is high in potassium and it helps things to bloom well.

There's a great tendency not to prune things, but pruning actually stimulates growth as well as tidying it up and stopping the plant getting leggy. Gardening books will help – I use the RHS ones, as they are generously illustrated and written in a way that is easy to understand and follow.

FREQUENTLY USED GARDENING TERMS

These are simple once you have mastered them.

ANNUAL

Plants with a life cycle of a year or one growing season.

PERENNIAL

Plants that live for a minimum of three seasons.

DECIDUOUS

Plants that shed their leaves at the end of the year or growing season, but renew them the following year.

EVERGREEN

Plants that keep their leaves for more than one growing season.

ERICACEOUS

Plants that like acid soil and dislike alkaline soil containing lime or chalk.

MULCH

Plant material applied to the soil surface to preserve moisture and maintain a cool temperature for plant roots.

VEGETABLES

If you want to try your hand at growing your own vegetables, then my main advice would be to grow what you like to eat. Make use of what space you have – you don't necessarily need a large area, and lots of veg (leeks, potatoes, courgettes, carrots and French beans) can be grown in deep pots, with runner beans and tomatoes in troughs against a wall. Shade isn't ideal, so try and find a spot that gets a good few hours of sunlight every day.

Herbs are such a joy: even if you don't have outside space, a few pots in your kitchen or on a windowsill – basil, parsley and chives, say – look lovely and can be used to perk up any dish. If you have room outside, you can plant hardy herbs like rosemary, sage and thyme.

RAISED BEDS

Raised beds are brilliant; I'm very keen on them because they're easy to manage, you can walk round them, control the feeding, weed them easily, and put good soil in them.

Make sure you have a path around raised beds and between them. Grass is difficult to mow if the space is too narrow – gravel or bark chips are better.

WEEDS

Weeds need to be dealt with, and you need to know what you're doing before attempting to deal with them. Perennial weeds are a real nuisance because they can cling on to life for several years: something like bindweed, with its trumpet-shaped white flowers, which winds itself around other plants, has to be dug out (and it can be hard work to do so!). Ground elder is another really bad one.

All you can do is dig out the roots and any shoots that are still there, use a weedkiller, then cover the affected area with black polythene, which prevents any light getting through and should therefore, in theory, stop growth. Let a year pass, and you will find that it does help. Luckily, most everyday weeds aren't so tricky to deal with, as long as you keep on top of your weeding regularly.

LAWNS

There is a lot to consider before you invest in a new
lawn. A healthy lawn requires a good amount of sun,
moisture and drainage – so if your garden is north-
facing and on clay soil, then it might involve more
upkeep than you realize. Always seek advice from the
garden centre before choosing a lawn: some types are
beautiful but not very hardwearing, so they won't last
long if you have a young family. If you've got a little
garden and you want a lawn, consider that you will
need somewhere to store the lawnmower, so if space
is at a premium it may not be quite the thing to
choose. However, if you're willing to put in the time,
lawns are a lovely thing to have; they add softness to
a garden in a way that artificial turf or a patio can't.

PLANTS

If you are planting new plants, look after them;
it's no good putting plants in if you don't water them.
Bought plants have got to be watered regularly, and
shrubs have to be watered in for the first year.

The best time of year to plant is when the ground has warmed up in spring, or in the autumn. When planting bare-rooted roses, autumn is best.

Many perennials can be divided (carefully lifted, chopped in half or divided with a fork, then replanted) in autumn to give you new plants the following spring.

Choose plants that have the look, colour and scent you like, and always plant in groups of three or five – uneven numbers look better; anything too symmetrical looks wrong.

The best times to water are first thing in the morning and last thing at night, as the plants can better absorb the water before it is lost to evaporation. For many people, a trusty watering can is quite sufficient, but an outdoor hose will save you an awful lot of trouble if you have a large area to cover. A sprinkler system that waters plants or pots on a timer is also a great help for when you're busy or not at home regularly. If you have the room, use a water butt to collect rainwater for your plants.

If you're sowing seeds, do so in a designated area, or mark out where you've sown them with a label, or some sand, so you don't go and weed out what you've sown!

GARDENING EQUIPMENT

You can gradually build up the kit that you need, but the following items are a good place to start:

SECATEURS / A TROWEL

A GOOD FORK & A SPADE

GARDENING GLOVES / BUCKETS

A WATERING CAN / A RAKE

COMPOST

Unless you have a very small garden, making your own compost is an efficient and environmentally friendly way of dealing with your kitchen and garden waste (see pages 85–6 for more on recycling kitchen waste), and a cost-effective way of enhancing your soil. You can buy a variety of wooden and plastic compost bins and containers in a range of sizes from garden centres now, and some local councils offer discounts, so it's easy to get started!

What to compost: Raw vegetable waste, dead flowers, lawn mowings and prunings.

What NOT to compost: Citrus peel doesn't break down, and cooked food is no good, plus it will bring rats – and you don't want that.

How to compost really depends on your composting receptacle and the time of year you begin the process: the warmth of summer means that any compost started then will come on more quickly than that started later in the year. Generally, though, making a good compost can take between 6 months and a couple of years.

I once heard someone describe making compost as being like making a cake – it's certainly true that the quantities you add are important, and that you need to do a certain amount of mixing . . .

WATER

I love the sound of moving water; we have a pond, but you can get all sorts of other water features. In the days when our local village fair used to give out goldfish in bags, everybody whose children got fed up with their fish used to put them into our pond. Goldfish can become very big when living in a large area of water, and you might even be able to call the fish in our pond carp now!

If you do want a pond, consider the age of your children, if you have any. It's not a good idea to have a pond if you have small children or are likely to have small children visiting – or, if you do, you must make sure it's fenced off safely (the same goes for swimming pools).

BIRD FEEDERS

It's lovely to have bird feeders in your garden, and I hang mine where I can see them, high up where cats can't get at them. I also hang them independently, like a hanging basket (not on the side of a tree or on top of a post), so that the squirrels can't reach them. The Royal Society for the Protection of Birds advises that sparrows and finches like seeds and thrushes and robins dried fruit, but protect your bird feeder, pay attention, and you will soon start to learn what each type of bird likes. (NB: dried fruit is poisonous for dogs, so take care if you have any!) A bird bath is another lovely feature as well as a place for birds to drink and wash.

WILDLIFE

There are lots of ways to encourage more wildlife into your garden; flowers that have high amounts of pollen and nectar are perfect for attracting bees and butterflies, while a pond of any size provides a habitat for frogs and newts. If you have the space, it can be wonderful to keep a slightly less tidy area of your garden reserved for growing wildflowers: it not only looks very nice but is also not much hassle to maintain. Creating habitats for animals, such as a log or leaf shelter for hedgehogs to hibernate in, is also a great activity to get children involved with.

FLOWERS

A vase of flowers, to me, means home. I think a house without fresh flowers and plants is without heart; if I've been away, the very first thing I do when I come home, after dumping my luggage, is put a bunch of flowers on the kitchen table. I love them, and I'm lucky that my husband does too. And they needn't be expensive or extravagant (though they can be). Before going out to buy flowers, look and see if there is an interesting shrub, some greenery or heather, a few buddleia or geranium heads, in your garden. Is there an interesting mahonia (an evergreen shrub) with its lovely yellow flowers, or have you got wisteria up the front of the house? A few heads of wisteria in a small vase or jug look good. Tough herbs like rosemary that need pruning anyway also look marvellous when in flower, as does lavender.

Whether you're buying them from a shop, or a market stall, or cutting them from your own garden, I think it's very good to remember the seasons; it's really sad to see a bunch of chrysanths in spring. I love jugs of mixed flowers, although it's also quite fun to have all one colour sometimes, if I'm picking from the garden. Other people might prefer a mixture of jazzy colours. If that's what you want to do, go for it. Everybody's different. I don't like some flowers, but other people might think they're heaven. The main thing really is to make sure they're in season: it's a great way to teach young children to know when things come around. And if you haven't got flowers, a big bowl of fruit on the table looks a bit different: lemons and a few bay leaves, say, or little gourds in autumn.

WINTER

Evergreens (such as **holly**, **ivy** and **firs**) are great for decorating the mantelpiece and table. **Poinsettias** are also festive-looking and readily available.

Red and white **amaryllis** last well cut and as flowering bulbs. To make a statement, grow three bulbs in one pot, cover with moss and support with twigs.

Hellebores (Christmas roses): seal the ends by dipping them into boiling water. I find that the very best way with hellebores is to float all the heads in a big, wide, shallow dish – or even a soup bowl. That's a really lovely one for when you have people around for supper, because it lasts well. Hellebores also look wonderful in pots outside the front door: you can get them in bud from garden centres just before Christmas, and they're lovely.

SPRING

I start off in early spring with those lovely paperwhite **narcissi**; they have the most wonderful smell, and it really makes me think spring's here. Grow them yourself in pots inside; paperwhites are not hardy, so it is unlikely they will grow again if you replant them outside.

Nothing says spring like **daffodils**, and what a pleasure it always is to see them, welcoming in the new season – it makes you feel there's joy to come. Always buy daffodils when they're still in bud; if you're picking them from the garden, make sure they're just about to open.

The life of **tulips** after cutting has improved over the years and they actually grow taller when put into water.

When picked in bud, the shrub **forsythia** will open with a blaze of yellow flowers: I love to watch it bloom in a jug.

Potting your own spring bulbs like **hyacinths**, **grape hyacinths** and **crocuses** is great and I love to do them. Plant several of the same kind in one pot for a wonderful display.

Every year at Easter I pick some twigs from the garden that are just about to open, like **hazel twigs**, and hang Easter eggs and little fluffy chickens off them. It's become a bit of a thing, the Easter tree, and the grandchildren love it.

SPRING: *A pot of primroses by a guest's bed makes them feel you thought about them.*

SUMMER

Alstroemeria are wonderfully long-lasting: grown at home they will go on flowering all summer until the frosts. When picking them, gently pull the stem out of the base of the plant, then cut to size. More flowers will come from the base.

Even just three **roses** picked in bud and placed in a vase look good.

Gladioli: These tall flowers are very high impact, so you only need a few in a narrow-necked vase. If you pull out the very top bud, it means that the rest of the top will flower – otherwise they have a tendency not to.

Sweet peas look and smell wonderful – if you haven't many, mix them with **Alchemilla mollis** (lady's mantle).

AUTUMN

Penstemons – though they don't last long once picked.

Little pot plants of **cyclamen**, grouped together, are lovely.

Small spray **chrysanthemums**.

Asters (Michaelmas daisies).

BUYING OR CUTTING FLOWERS & MAKING THEM LAST

When you buy flowers regularly, you soon find out what lasts and what doesn't. There are certain things that florists tend to pop into a bunch that really don't have any longevity: lisianthus and sprigs of mint are two that spring to mind.

Roses have been bred to last much longer than they used to – they should keep for a week – and are always lovely.

Lilies also last well and are now often bred without stamens. Whether you've bought them or grown them yourself, if your lilies have stamens, do remember to keep cutting them out as soon as they open and put them straight into the compost bin. Otherwise you'll be sure to walk past in a pale shirt and the pollen will get on it (see page 228 for what to do if this happens!) – and it's very difficult to get out.

It's best to pick flowers from the garden either first thing in the morning or as the sun goes down. If you are planning to use them with florist's foam in an arrangement, put the picked flowers into a bucket of water and leave them in a cool place for the day or overnight to soak up as much water as possible. For tulips, wrap the stems tightly in paper and stand them in water overnight in a cold place. Next day remove the paper and put them into a vase – if you do this, they will not drop. Amaryllis have hollow stems, so if you are using them in an arrangement, insert wooden support sticks inside the stem. The cut stems tend to curl up after a few days, so tape the base with sticky tape to keep them firm and sturdy.

> *Always remove any leaves below the water level in the vase; any leaves sitting in the water will make it turn green and smell!*

Use flower food if you like, or if some comes with your bunch of flowers. Some people say to put a dash of sugar in the water; on their website the RHS give details of how to make your own homemade plant food from water, sugar, vinegar and bleach, though they advise that it is unlikely to work as well as the stuff you buy.

An old piece of wisdom to help cut flowers last longer is to put a copper penny or an aspirin in the water, because they are thought to prevent bacteria growing. I haven't tested this under scientific conditions, but some people swear by it!

TIPS FOR ARRANGING

Trends come and go, in flowers as in all things, and very 'arranged' flowers are no longer as popular as they have previously been – though of course this will probably change again. Even so, some of the principles of flower-arranging are worth thinking about, or at least having at the back of your mind:

Wash your vases thoroughly (see pages 63–4) and remember to change the water – how often you need to do this will depend on your flowers, but generally it will be every few days or when it doesn't look or smell fresh.

Chop around 5cm off the bottom of the stalks, at an angle: this helps the flowers take the water up. If they start to look a bit sad, remove any dead ones and trim the remaining flowers again – this will help them to last a little bit longer.

The flowers should be one and a half times taller/higher than the height of the vase.

The width (i.e. the furthest points of your greenery on either side) should be double the width of the vase or receptacle/container.

You should have a tall/high flower in the middle of the arrangement, and then fill in around it.

POLLEN

Beware of pollen on clothes, particularly lily pollen, as it stains terribly. If you do get some on your clothes, immediately blow away as much as you can, then dab it once with a piece of sticky tape to lift off the excess. Then treat with stain remover.

VASES, JUGS & JARS

There's nothing nicer than having a big-impact vase of something on a table to really wow, but a little vase of two or three stems is also terribly effective.

- Tall flowers – delphiniums, lilies, gladioli – need tall vases. If you have bought or been given a bunch that are too short for your vase and they are wrapped in film or plastic, you can scrunch it up and put it into the bottom of the vase before adding water and the stems will sit happily on top. Alternatively, you can add pebbles or gravel, allowing the flowers to sit at the right height.

- All flower arrangements on dinner tables should be either low enough to enable you to see over the top when you're sitting down – or very, very tall, so that you can see through them. Otherwise you won't be able to see the person on the other side of the table!

- Some vases are better than others for keeping arrangements together. The ones that slope outward at the top are very

common but can make the flowers wilt or cause large gaps in the centre. I have recently discovered fishbowl vases, which are a good solution as they not only look very attractive but also help to keep flowers standing up like soldiers.

- Some people don't like to see the stems in clear glass vases, and a good short-term solution to this is to line the inside of the glass with aspidistra or other large leaves.

It's lovely to have different vases and jugs, but your kitchen can throw up a number of DIY vases too, and there's nothing nicer than reusing something for the purpose it wasn't meant for!

- Jam jars (see page 64 for how to clean off their sticky labels) make lovely little vases, and a few sprigs of flowers, roses or herbs in a jam jar with a nice lemon or green bow round the top fits the bill.

- Glass spice pots and milk bottles can also be requisitioned and look very attractive placed in a line down a table, with a flower and a couple of bits of greenery/foliage in each.

- Deep tealight holders or shot glasses or Moroccan tea glasses make lovely small vases too.

CLEANING & STORING VASES & CONTAINERS

The dishwasher may turn good glass cloudy; for tips on how best to clean glass vases and containers see pages 63–4. In the case of china jugs or other flower containers, it's a good idea to use an old non-wire scouring pad to clean the inside, because some leaves and other bits will inevitably have stuck to it. You can also add a little squirt of bleach and then rinse it, and that will disinfect it very well – make sure to rinse it out thoroughly (although florists often add a little sprinkle of bleach to their water).

If you have a lot of jugs and containers and you do want to store them, it's a good idea to keep them in a shallow cupboard, so you don't have trouble getting to the ones at the back. Anything you're not going to use very often – such as containers for bulbs which you might use just once a year – can be stored in the garage, attic, cellar, or other non-prime real estate storage space.

Storing vases and things can be a nightmare, because they come in odd shapes and sizes – although this is what makes them so useful for displaying a range of flowers! It may seem terribly obvious, but it does make sense to buy vases or jugs that you like the look of so that you can leave them out on display, whether it's on a shelf, a dresser, or the kitchen worktop. If your vases or jugs are lovely and decorative, there's no reason why they can't live in their respective spots all the time, whether they are filled with flowers or not!

HOUSEPLANTS

Plants come with instructions and you should always read them – or do some research – before investing. If all your windowsills are very sunny, you don't want to end up buying something like a primula that shouldn't be in direct sunlight. If you keep a succulent in a bathroom that has no windows, then, as a desert plant, it isn't going to thrive (ferns, such as Boston ferns, on the other hand, do well in bathrooms, as they like a humid atmosphere). Errors like these can be avoided by reading the instructions, though sometimes it's only through personal trial and error that we learn this!

Some people are very clever with orchids and they're great to have as a houseplant. They don't want to be in direct sunlight, they want to be watered once a week, fed from time to time, and kept at an even temperature (depending on the variety, this can vary from 10°C to 18°C).

I also love streptocarpus, which are houseplants with great long leaves and beautiful little flowers that come in pink, white or blue at the end of a long stem. They do need light, but should be kept out of direct sunlight and at an even room temperature. To propagate them, you cut the leaf and put it straight down into the soil to get new ones.

WINDOW BOXES

If you don't have a garden and houseplants aren't practical, planting window boxes can be a lovely way to try your hand at gardening and bring some colour to your home.

Hardy plants such as geraniums or herbs like rosemary and thyme tend to do well: use a mixture of perennials and annuals that can be replaced, but work out first whether the area is sunny or shady and choose your plants accordingly.

Measure your exterior windowsills and make sure they are deep enough for your chosen box or pots to sit safely.

What style you choose is up to you, but a low box or pot will be more stable than a taller one – if your sill is at a height, remember that your plants will be exposed to the wind.

Make sure your container has holes for water to drain through. Line with a thin layer of shards of broken terracotta pots or old pebbles to prevent the holes getting clogged up with compost.

Water and prune plants according to the instructions, deadheading any old flower heads or yellowing leaves as necessary to keep them looking smart.

HOSTING &
ADDING THE EXTRA TOUCHES

Worth doing well

'Do as much as you can in terms of preparing the food in advance – then you don't have to worry about it when everyone arrives.'

DINNER PARTIES

There's nothing I like more than entertaining friends and family. Generally, this means cooking, so food is important, but what matters most, to me at least, is how you look after your guests. For this reason, it's a good idea to do as much as you can in terms of preparing the food in advance – then you don't have to worry about it when everyone arrives and you can actually spend time with your friends. There's nothing worse than having people over, not having things ready and not being able to focus on anything but the food.

If the food side of entertaining really worries you, keep it very simple. Make the most of your freezer: it can take a huge amount of stress out of the day to know that your food is already prepared and just needs to be defrosted. For lunch, fresh bread, good cheeses and chutneys are delicious. You mustn't stress or panic about entertaining, because the whole point of having people over is to have fun. Don't ever feel guilty. If you don't cook, you can cheat, and do it with skill and panache. And build on your strengths: if you have beautiful flowers in your garden, or love arranging them, go to town on the flowers!

TWO GOLDEN RULES TO CONSIDER

Having friends and family round to your house, whether it's for a meal or to stay, is a matter of being organized.

———

Choose a menu that you can cope with, for the number of guests you're having, and choose both hot and cold food to make preparation easier.

THE TABLE

TABLEWARE

How much crockery you need depends on how you like to host.

As a general rule of thumb, you can't go wrong by making sure you have the same number of dinner plates as you have places for people to sit around the table. If you're going to have people round more informally and they might sit on the sofas or a stool, or stand, it makes sense to have more bowls than plates, because you can eat out of a bowl more easily with a spoon and fork.

If you like crockery to match, that's lovely, but if you're tight on room you probably don't need a cereal bowl, a soup bowl, a dessert bowl and a pasta bowl. It can be equally nice to have mismatching plates and bowls: it's really a matter of personal taste.

Sizes have changed over the years but a dinner plate is generally around 26–28cm. A bread plate should be around 15cm.

DRINKS & GLASSWARE

Labelling wine

You can get slate tags that you can write on with chalk, which are very nice, or wipe-clean ones: write the wine and the year on the front of the bottle (so you don't have to pull it out each time to see what it is), and on the back, as well as who gave it to you, if it was a gift, and when. This is a nice way to remember being given something special – and it also ensures you don't give something back to the person who gave it to you!

GLASSES

What type of glasses you use will depend on your household and what you like, but here are some of the main varieties it can be useful to have:

Water/everyday tumblers – those made with recycled glass are slightly thicker and very robust.

Red wine – these should be large, so the wine can breathe.

Shot – these can also be used for serving little puddings in.

Plastic – these are best when eating outside, to prevent accidents.

Champagne flutes or saucers – Flutes are classic tall style while saucers are more bowl-shaped.

Beer – traditionally in a half-pint mug, but a large glass will do.

White wine – if I have room in the fridge, I chill my glass so it's lovely and frosty and my wine stays cold for longer.

Brandy – a wide bowl shape, narrower at the top.

Sherry and Port – smaller than a wine glass to encourage more restrained drinking!

Martini – v-shaped glass on a stem, for cocktails or spirit-mixed drinks.

Highball – perfect for soft or long drinks.

FORMAL PLACE SETTINGS

Cutlery should be placed in the order in which you will use it, so a smaller knife and fork on the outside for the first course, then a larger size on the inside. If you have them, fish and/or steak knives can be substituted for the larger knife, depending on what you are eating.

Soup spoons, if soup is being served, should be placed to the right.

Small dessertspoons and forks should be placed above the plate, with the handle of the fork pointing to the left and that of the spoon to the right, above the fork. Dessertspoons should be picked up with your right hand, dessert forks with your left. In America, the spoon and fork are placed alongside the knife and fork, next to the plate.

Side plates should be placed to the left, with a butter knife on top of the plate.

Napkins can be placed to the left (beside or underneath the forks), or in the middle of each place setting.

Glasses should be placed to the right, sitting above the knives; the water glass should be placed furthest in (i.e. furthest from reach).

*Serve guests from the **left**,
clear plates from the **right**,
and remove the salt and pepper
from the table after
the main course.*

INFORMAL

Stand knives and forks in a nice jug: People can pick them up along with their napkins and that's fine.

Platters are a sociable and informal way of serving food, as they encourage interaction. Do make sure to provide sensibly sized serving utensils, though – very large ones mean that people will help themselves to more and you don't want everything to go too quickly. Some people may want seconds!

Glasses: Instead of the traditional three glasses, we tend to lay the table with one water glass and one wine glass now, and then put the second glass on the side, because sometimes people stay with the wine that they've started with. Anything to save on the washing up!

TABLE EXTRAS

Decant salt and pepper into little containers so that people can help themselves, and condiments like mustard (English, whole-grain and Dijon) or horseradish into little bowls with small spoons.

It's always good to have plenty of bread for those with big appetites, and even nicer if you serve it warm.

I put a fresh piece of butter in a butter dish; I love to use good butter and prefer unsalted, though this is a matter of personal taste.

Flowers are lovely: they must be either high or low enough so that you can see the person opposite you and are able to talk to them. See page 226 for more on flowers.

A tablecloth is very nice, but mats are fine too. If your table is precious, use a protector or place mats underneath the cloth. If the thought of cleaning a starched white table-cloth seems daunting, go for a coloured or patterned one (the latter can be particularly forgiving when it comes to spillages). A piece of fabric will do the job just as well as a tablecloth, as long as it's the right size. Covering a long table with kraft paper can also look very nice for less formal meals, and is great for children; give them some soft crayons that won't damage your table and let them scribble away!

LAYING OUT A BUFFET

The key is to place everything in the order
in which people should take it:

1. Plates or bowls should be at the beginning of the table so people can take these first.

2. The main dish should be laid out next to these – if you are serving something like a pie, lasagne or a whole poached fish, you may want to score out the portion sizes lightly to help your guests (otherwise people can be unsure how much to take!). Make sure there are serving utensils alongside.

3. Side dishes, salads, sauces, condiments and seasonings should be next. It's nice to have a basket of bread, cut into small pieces, too.

4. Place cutlery in a jug alongside a stack of napkins at the end of the table – alternatively, wrap napkins around knives and forks to make them easier to carry. Either way, if they are at the end then no one should forget them!

Guests often like to tear off chunks of bread in a size to suit them, but it's not very hygienic. Wrapping loaves in linen napkins will protect them from hands, and keep fresh bread warm and prevent it from drying out.

THINKING AHEAD

Treat having guests sort of like a play: Whether they're there for the evening or the weekend, think ahead to all the acts, make notes and have everything ready so that when the curtain goes up, you're set.

Consider how many people you want to invite: This may well dictate what kind of meal you can serve. Why not make something you're confident with? Eating has become informal: it's worth remembering that it doesn't have to be grand and it doesn't have to be expensive. There's nothing wrong with a nice macaroni cheese with tomatoes, or a good casserole. People love home-cooked food – nothing too complicated. All-in-one or one-pot dishes like lasagne, shepherd's or cottage pie, fish pie, or casseroles and stews are great, as you can prepare them in advance – and they cut down on the washing-up!

Times have changed, and it's quite usual now to email and ask your guests if they have any allergies or other food requirements. If you are the recipient of such an email, make sure to read it – and then to reply. It's easy to forget, but this does put your host on the spot some-what, and if there's something you can't eat then your meal may be rather cobbled together – for which you only have yourself to blame!

It's worth keeping a list of close friends and family and making a note of who is vegetarian, who doesn't eat kiwi fruit and so on. Stick it on the back of a cupboard door or in your diary – because if you see them often, it's nice not to have to ask. People are always terribly touched when you remember to do things like provide gluten-free bread, for example, if they are coeliac.

When you're confident you have all the information you need to settle on your menu, plan your cooking times and what needs to go into the oven when: Unless you have a double oven, it's a good idea to spread out the cooking between the stovetop and the oven, otherwise you might struggle. If you have an Aga, do as much as you can in the ovens, to save the heat.

Make a shopping list and work out what you need to buy from the shops in advance. If you need to visit your local bakery, butcher or fishmonger, think about when these are open and factor them into your planning. Fishmongers tend to shut on Sunday and Monday, so a fish pie may not be the most practical choice for a Monday night supper.

If you don't have a car, ordering online from your supermarket of choice and getting home delivery may be a good option, especially for heavy items like tins and bottles. Doing your shop in two stages is a good tip too: Get the bulk in advance, then do a final shop the day before or thereabouts. This way you'll be less likely to forget anything, and you can buy items that benefit from being fresh (salad, herbs and fruit for example), or pick up anything that you couldn't find originally at the last minute. Remember that online deliveries sometimes make substitutes, so it's wise to not leave this until the last minute and then find that they don't have something crucial in stock!

Drinks need as much consideration as the menu. If it's mid-winter and cold, offering a hot drink such as mulled wine is a nice touch and has the added benefit of smelling lovely. It's also very important to have interesting non-alcoholic drinks available, especially if you have guests who don't drink, are driving, or are pregnant (not to mention younger guests). Increasingly many people are choosing not to drink, and so there are a wide range of juices, cordials, flavoured sparkling waters and tonics available, plus a variety of low alcohol beers (0.5% and below).

Having set the table, I think it's very important to place people – otherwise you can end up with all the men at one end of the table and all the women at the other. With a formal table plan, traditionally the most important person should sit on the right of the host. I like to think about who would get on well and plan the seating accordingly. If you have a couple with one partner who is very shy or doesn't know anyone, they may like to be seated next to each other. Ideally, you wouldn't always sit children next to their parents but this is such a personal thing, and will depend on the individuals involved and their age. Sometimes, if you're a crowd, it works well to sit all the children on one table. Do what works for you. Whichever way you want to do it, you should start thinking about where you are going to seat everyone at least a few days in advance – it's part of the pleasure of looking forward to the evening. And write the order down! If you try to do it just before your guests arrive, you'll be sure to get it wrong.

ON THE DAY

1

Chilling drinks: This is very important and takes longer than you think, especially if you consider that you're going to be opening the fridge door a lot. Put champagne, white and sparkling wine, beer and anything else that needs to be cold into the fridge early. Unless you have an ice-maker fridge-freezer, it's useful to tip ice out of its trays, and put it into a big container or an ice bucket so that you have lots ready. Do this in advance: you won't want to be rattling round with the ice just before your guests arrive. Remember, if chilling bottles in tubs with ice, the labels will come off. Which means you won't be able to return them if you've got them on sale or return. Sit bottles on top of the ice and make sure they don't get wet by pouring away any excess melted water – or cover the ice with a clean cloth or tea towel and sit the bottles on top of that.

② **Setting the table:** I love to make the table look lovely with candles and flowers and what have you, but what you cook will dictate how you serve it up, to an extent. Laying a table does take time, and if you're in a hurry or if it's an informal affair, there's no need to get out the silverware and do a full formal setting. See page 241 for more on setting the table.

③ **Place settings:** If there are a lot of people, name places are very useful. Children love to make these: they draw a tennis racquet for Mum's friend who plays tennis, or a rugby ball for somebody who plays rugby; it keeps them out of mischief and makes them a part of it all. Anagrams of people's names are fun too.

④ **Heating plates:** Hot plates are immensely important to me, because a meal can take time to eat, and it's nice when it's hot. But to some people it doesn't matter at all, and in France they nearly always have cold plates. It really does depend on what you like and how you're serving. Plating up food individually means that it will lose heat more quickly: a plate of pasta or a Sunday roast both tend to cool rapidly, so you might consider heating the plates when serving these, even if it's not something you usually do. If you want to heat your plates, it's advisable to get them going well before your guests arrive. There are lots of ways to do this: put them in the oven on a low heat, in an empty dishwasher on a very short wash, or run them under hot water, then dry them.

⑤ **Accepting help:** If you're playing host to great friends, they will often want to lend a hand, whether it's passing snacks round, helping you to carry things from the kitchen, pouring drinks, or even washing up. Whether you accept is entirely up to you and depends on how you feel, but it's worth remembering that often people like being helpful (especially if they are solo), and it can be better to accept help when you need it rather than struggle to do everything by yourself and neglect your guests.

COOKING ON THE SPOT

The most important part of hosting is looking after your guests and spending time with them. You shouldn't be running around chopping vegetables and making sauces when people have arrived, but there are simple things that can be cooked while your guests are there. Stir-fries are cooked very quickly at a high heat and should be eaten as soon as they're done – they do not improve with age or benefit from pre-cooking! That's not to say that you can't prepare them thoroughly in advance, though – you can have every ingredient chopped and marinated and ready to go (this is what chefs mean when they talk about *mise en place* or 'everything in its place'). If you're eating in the kitchen and your guests are sitting happily with drinks in their hands, as soon as you're ready to eat you can just set to and throw everything in the wok and everyone will be delighted.

Barbecuing is another good example of simple cooking that can be done when your guests are there. Preparation is what it's all about: apart from having your meat and other bits marinated, the most crucial part of being an organized barbecuer is working out when you need to have the fire ready with a traditional charcoal fire. In my experience, this always takes longer than you think it will. You can buy a barbecue chimney starter, where the coals are heated in a container before being poured on to the barbecue, and that can save you a lot of time. As soon as the coals reach the stage where they are glowing and perfect for cooking over, you should have everything ready to go – if you don't, you run the risk of missing the moment, and having to rebuild the fire! Gas barbecues are easier to get going, but it is essential to set the grill rack at the right height. When buying a barbecue, I always think it's nice to have space at the sides to keep food hot.

CANAPÉS

- Serve a mixture of vegetarian and meat and fish, bread and pastry-based things and lighter bites, and hot and cold – think about what you need the oven for, and don't overload it.

- Think of different types of presentation – pieces of slate, wooden boards, trays, different-shaped plates, bowls, baskets, and leaves used to line plates make the canapés look exciting and different.

- Ask your guests to help you pass platters round.

- Consolidate half-empty plates or platters and arrange the food prettily on one plate.

- Place cocktail sticks for spearing (e.g. mini sausages) in a small glass – and put empty bowls out so that your guests have somewhere to place the sticks when they're done.

- Have small napkins to hand.

QUANTITIES

If you're serving a first course/starter: just 1–2 per person

If you're not serving a first course/starter: 3–4 per person

If it's a nibbles only drinks party: 8–10 per person

MAKING TEA & COFFEE

What can be nicer than finishing a lovely meal
with a selection of tea and coffee?

Warm the teapot first by pouring boiling water into it and swilling it round. Pour the water out, then make your tea. Add milk to china cups first, followed by tea. I know that this will be a source of great contention for those who believe in tea before milk (just as people feel very strongly about the order of jam and cream on a scone), but this is how I do things.

Always offer hot milk with coffee for guests who, like me, want really hot coffee!

CARRYING LOTS OF CUPS & SAUCERS

When I used to run Aga workshops in my kitchen and made tea and coffee for a large group, I learnt a trick for fitting 16 cups and saucers on one tray:

Place 4 saucers in a stack.

Lay the cups sideways on top of the saucers, tucking a handle into the top of each so they all slot together and sit on the saucer space perfectly.

CALLING IT A NIGHT

Some people love people to stay on and on … but if you feel that you want to end the evening, you can give them a hint by gently starting to clear things away. My husband has been known to draw the curtains! A few comments like, 'Gosh, you've got to go to work tomorrow morning!' or 'Shall we find you a cab number?' or 'Do you think you're going to stay – if so, we'll open another bottle, otherwise we won't bother?' The last one is particularly good because people usually say, 'Oh no, it's time to go!' If you know people are going to stay very late, you can also pre-empt it by asking them round earlier, if it's not a weeknight. If you are a night owl, take no notice of any of this. With really close friends, I just say 'OK, time's up!'

HOUSE GUESTS

HAVING PEOPLE TO STAY OVERNIGHT OR FOR THE WEEKEND

When you have people coming to stay and you know that you're going to do something like go for a long walk, make sure to tell them before they come so that they can bring boots and the right kind of clothes. If they have children, think of some activities for them too (a puzzle or a colouring book or something – I collect things – or a treasure hunt outside), so they don't have to resort to playing on tablets!

Make sure the bed is well aired, with clean sheets.

If they're cold mortals, they will probably appreciate a hot-water bottle or an electric blanket.

Flowers are always a lovely touch and show that you have thought of your guest.

In the bathroom: fresh towels, nice things for the bath and, if you think they would appreciate it, a candle with matches alongside. I also have a little box with a face flannel, ear plugs, cotton wool and cotton buds, moisturizer, hairbrush and comb, a new toothbrush and mini toothpaste – the sort of things one tends to need but also to forget.

By the bed: a bottle of water, something to read and a torch. (We once had somebody to stay who was going for a very important job interview for which he had to leave at 5 a.m., and we had an electricity cut in the night. Fortunately we had candles and matches, and a torch – otherwise however would you manage in a strange house? It might not seem like something that would happen, but it's well worth thinking about.)

Tell your guests about any idiosyncrasies with the water. You know, if it takes a while to warm up or whatever, otherwise they'll think there's no hot water! I stick a little note in the bathroom, saying, 'Takes a long time for the water to come through, be patient.'

PLAN THE NEXT MORNING

Decide before your guests go to bed what time you're going to have breakfast and what your loose plans for the day are. Obviously, these don't have to be set in stone, but it's useful to know so that you can dress accordingly. If you have a dog and take it for an early morning walk, ask your guests if they'd like to join you before breakfast. Then they can say no – at least that's what happens in my house.

Prepare a tray of tea and coffee that your guests can make themselves in their room (remember to give them a jug of milk before they go to bed – I always forget to do that), or, if you don't have room for that, leave everything out on a tray in the kitchen so that they can help themselves if they're up early.

PLAN YOUR MEALS

When people come to stay and you've got time, you can really go for it on the breakfast front: eggs, bacon, black pudding, kippers . . . It's worth considering that you might not be hungry for lunch if you have a cooked breakfast, so if that's on the cards, something lighter might be more sensible. I always think it's a good idea to have a very light lunch, and then you can go to town in the evening.

FREEZING: DISHES FOR OCCASIONS

Whether you have guests for dinner or for the weekend, you probably don't want to spend very much time cooking when they're there. Think about what you are going to eat, and choose things that freeze really well. If you've got a gang of children coming, nobody will say no to a first-rate lasagne – you can do all the prep and cooking in advance and, on the day, thaw it and put it straight into the oven.

Cottage pie is another good option/crowd pleaser, although the potato topping should only be frozen for a short period of time, say a week in advance.

Something like an empty blind-baked, or even raw, quiche case is frightfully useful. For a lovely homemade lunch, all you need to do is take it out and allow it time to defrost, then fry a few onions and sliced bacon, add some eggs and cream and pop it into the oven, and you'll have a freshly baked quiche.

If you love to bake, and are planning to make roulade or a meringue, well, you might just as well make two and keep one ready for the next time you've got people coming round. (Pack the meringue carefully, so it doesn't get crushed.) Crumble, cheesecakes and cakes are all great to freeze too.

Soups freeze very well, especially those that are puréed. In winter, we tend to eat much more of them; nothing is more warming on a frosty day, so it's always worth having some stored away in your freezer. All you really need to do to bring them to life is add a dollop of cream before serving. Croutons are always a wonderful addition to a bowl of soup and, if you have a stale loaf of bread, it's a really good idea to make a big batch and divide them up in packets. Then, next time you have soup, you can just drop them in.

'Whether you have guests for dinner or for the weekend, you probably don't want to spend very much time cooking when they're there. Think about what you are going to eat, and choose things that freeze really well.'

THE EXTRA TOUCHES: GIFTS

THE GIFT OF GIVING

When you go to a friend's house for dinner, it's usual to bring a bottle of wine, a box of chocolates, or maybe some flowers. Even if I am being taken out to lunch, I pretty much always take the host a small something. While you can buy lovely things, I do love to bring a homemade gift: it means such a lot, as you are giving your time and thought. It's a very special thing. That said, you should always think of who you are giving to, and what they might like and find useful. Useful gifts are terribly underrated. Another good rule of thumb – obvious but still worth pointing out – is only to give a gift you'd wish to receive yourself.

Remember too that gifts needn't be expensive. Sometimes the most valuable thing you can give is your time: an evening's baby-sitting for new parents, or a day out . . . these sorts of things mean an awful lot.

EDIBLE GIFTS

Take the trouble to label any edible gifts nicely and with some detail: say what they are, if they need to be refrigerated (curd, for example, does) and the date that they were made, so the recipient knows when to eat them by!

- **Lemon curd**
- **Chutney**
- **Jam**
- **Homemade honey is a lovely gift – especially if you're a beekeeper!**
- **Fruit vinegars (see page 106)**
- **Sloe gin**
- **Fudge or Scottish tablet**
- **Meringue kisses**
- **Shortbread or little biscuits**
- **Cheese straws (see page 91)**

ARTS AND CRAFTS

If you're good at a craft, like sewing or knitting, then why not put this into practice. Try to make things that have a specific use – ornamental gifts, though lovely, have a tendency to gather dust, or linger in drawers . . .

Little bags of dried lavender are quick and fairly straightforward to make; tuck them into your underwear or nightwear drawer, or with your jumpers to make everything smell nice.

A knitted tea cosy is an ambitious project; knitted fire mitts are simpler, and a very useful gift for anyone with an open fire.

FLOWERS

Before buying or arranging a large bunch of flowers, consider that your host might have gone to a lot of trouble to put flowers in the house already. A hand-picked posy can be popped into a jam jar with water – this not only looks terribly sweet, but it also spares your host the trouble of finding a vase.

If you can't get to a florist, and don't have flowers for picking in the garden, supermarkets often have a good range of seasonal flowers (see pages 218–26). To give them that extra finishing touch, take them out of their plastic covering and wrap them in some brown kraft paper tied with raffia or ribbon (see page 263). You can even add a little extra greenery if you have it: why not!

WRAP IT UP

I've got a present cupboard and collect things for it throughout the year. This might not be practical for everyone, but it works for me. What is useful is to have a place where you store gift cards (see below), tags, and any odd ribbons and bits of wrapping, so that everything is in one place.

A note on regifting: This is a matter of personal preference. If you would like to repurpose something that you haven't used and that you think someone else might enjoy or use, then by all means do – but it is advisable to put a label or make a note of who gave it to you originally, so you don't run the risk of giving something back to the person who gave it to you!

Requisition old glass jars for jams, curds, chutneys and pickles, sterilizing them and removing any sticky residue from the outside (see page 64) before using. Fill your jars as far up as you can: the principle of sealing is to exclude air, and this helps with that.

Fudge, biscuits, and cheese straws look nice in large glass preserving jars – and the recipient can use them afterwards, as a Brucie Bonus! Clear bags are also good and are inexpensive when bought in bulk.

Save odd ends of wrapping paper, fabric and even leftover wallpaper for covering the lids of jars.

Save the raffia or ribbon when you are given flowers or presents. Iron it and store it away – it looks lovely tied round jam jars, big glass jars or clear bags.

GIFT CARDS

A yearly wall planner calendar stuck on the back of a door or cupboard is a good idea: it's easy to forget to transfer dates over to your diary – and many people use digital diaries now anyway, but a chart is hard to miss. One year I was really organized and managed to get ahead of myself and buy all the cards for the year in order of when the birthdays fell – though I've never done it since!

It's not a bad idea to buy cards you like or that seem very appropriate to the recipient when you see them and stockpile them. Do put a label on them, though, so you know who they're intended for – and do keep them all in one place (I have a box specially for this), otherwise you are liable to thwart yourself and forget what you have!

If you have crafty inclinations, then of course you can make your own cards – and cards made by children are always a lovely thing. Personalized photo cards can also be very thoughtful, and older people are often fond of them.

There's nothing nicer than getting a card through the post, among all the bills, but when you do forget a birthday, e-cards are very useful for sending at the last minute and getting you out of trouble.

I save Christmas cards and birthday cards and give them to my grandchildren to make gift tags (though I keep special ones).

CORRESPONDENCE

Thank you letters are very much appreciated. More and more, people send an email, but to my mind, a card saying thank you after a meal or staying with someone is lovely. It doesn't need to be long or formal – you're not writing an essay! – but if you can just pick out one or two things that you specially enjoyed or that your host went to a lot of trouble for, that will make their day.

You don't have to buy an expensive card (though you may happen upon a card in a shop that's really quite funny or suitable for your host); I almost never buy thank you cards, because I would always rather write a short letter. Plus, buying a card specially can be a disincentive to sending the note, which isn't the point! The boxes of postcards that you can buy now are also good, if you see a type that you particularly like.

It's never too late to say thank you, but ideally you should send it fairly soon after the event in question: it means more, though even a note arriving a few weeks later will still be lovely and thoughtful. There's no need to send it first class unless you think the recipient will really be offended by being 'second class'; it's going to get there as long as you remember the postcode. Do put some thought into how the envelope looks; neat handwriting and a straight stamp are the kind of things that I always notice.

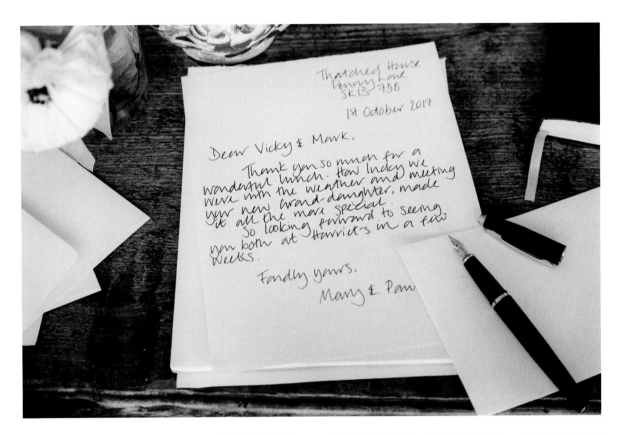

REPLYING TO INVITATIONS

Times are changing, and some invitations include a card that you fill in now, because people are so useless about RSVP-ing. The main thing is to do it promptly – think of the people who are organizing the party. It helps them to know how many people are coming. And read it carefully. If they want to know whether you don't like certain foods, or are allergic to foods, tell them.

PERSONAL CORRESPONDENCE

All of us will have something that happens in our lives that means we receive masses of letters and want to reply to them. When my son, Will, died, I had a concertina file where I kept people's letters of condolence. I organized them into those I had replied to, and those I hadn't yet replied to, and I kept them all because I wanted to re-read them – and I found that very useful.

CHRISTMAS

People tend to get really worried about Christmas, because they think it's an event and panic. But really, it is just a big family roast. Sit down with a large sheet of paper, not the back of an envelope, and make some lists: who's coming, how many days you've got people round, when you're going out, when you're staying in and so on . . . Once you know who's coming for what meals, and when you're likely to be out, you can do a little master plan (which can change, of course; it doesn't need to be set in stone – the point is that it means you don't end up over-buying). Christmas is an expensive time, so to spread the cost out, why not start early: buy tinned things, or things that have a long use-by date. Or non-perishables like red candles – something the shops always seem to run out of in December! It's all just a matter of organization.

Be realistic about what you can get done in the time you have available, and also don't feel guilty if you haven't time to do things: you can buy them. I always use frozen chestnuts, for example. If you can make things in advance that freeze well, like stuffing and the odd pud, by all means do. It'll give you peace of mind.

A NOTE ON CHRISTMAS COOKING

It's really all a matter of being organized, but these are my two top tips:

Order your turkey in advance, or, if you have a frozen one, be sure to allow time for it to defrost (see page 22).

Make as much as possible ahead, to give yourself less to do on the day: bread sauce and stuffing (in a tin, or a roasting dish) can both be made the day before, then refrigerated and reheated on the day. Cranberry sauce can also be made in advance, or bought.

CLEMENTINES AND ORANGES

Clementines and oranges are a favourite around Christmas-time, and the peel has a variety of uses. Citrus-flavoured sugar can be created simply by adding the dried peel to a jar of granulated sugar and leaving it to infuse. Dried peel also burns very well in an open fire and gives a lovely smell, or you can make homemade potpourri by adding it to a bowl along with cinnamon sticks, pine cones and star anise.

To dry citrus peel:

1. Peel off the rind with a serrated peeler, avoiding the white pith.

2. Place the peel flat on top of a low radiator or at the back of an Aga, or on a piece of kitchen paper in an airing cupboard for a few days, until dried.

DECORATIONS

When you put up your Christmas decorations is a personal thing and will probably depend on how busy you are from year to year. If you've got children, chances are you will be nagged to do it from the 1st of December! The second weekend of December is quite nice, but it's all about when you've got the time.

THE TREE

If you're having a fresh cut Christmas tree, Nordmann firs are less likely to drop their needles than Norway spruces, but are more expensive.

Work out how tall you want your tree to be (this will depend on your ceiling height!), and think of the width of the space where you're going to put it, too. Ask the person you buy it from to chop the end off the trunk for you if it's a little too tall – chopping a little bit off the end so it's freshly cut will also help your tree to take in more water.

It's a very good idea to buy a stand that allows you to screw the end of your tree in place and that holds water. Top up the water daily to keep your tree nice and green – and try not to stand it too near a radiator or the fire, as these will both cause it to lose water and dry out more quickly.

How you decorate is totally up to you – personally, I love birds on the tree, red and silver, and a lot of things that the children have made. We've been through blue baubles and clever ideas, but that's what we do now. Christmas is all about memories and, for me, that extends to the decorations: I keep mine from year to year and still have little bells made out of egg boxes that my children made. I've given them two lots each, and of course they now say to their children, 'Look what Mummy and Daddy did when they were little.' It's lovely to make new memories by buying or giving baubles to mark special occasions, like a couple or baby's first Christmas. Then each year, when you bring them out, you can remember what they mark.

Remember not to hang anything edible low in the tree if you have animals, because chocolate Father Christmases wrapped in foil are delicious for a dog, and they can pull the tree over. It's just too tempting – for children too.

LIGHTS

I always used to pack my traditional filament lights away carefully; I'd write on the outside of the box the date and the fact that they were working – but I could have assured you that when I came to unpack them the following Christmas, they wouldn't be working any more . . . This is less of a problem with LED lights, which are increasingly common. LEDs are more expensive but they use less power, are less prone to breaking – and as they generate little heat, they are safer around furnishings.

You can buy very nice portable battery-operated lights that are perfect for table decoration or little trees; if you lower the lights when you have your Christmas meal, as we do, they look lovely dotted around.

If you have battery-operated lights, be sure to take the batteries out before packing them away.

DECORATING AROUND THE FIREPLACE

I have a piece of rope that I put over the top and down the sides of the mantelpiece, and I wire on foliage. Rather than buying it, trim the lower branches of the Christmas tree off and use those – or ask if they have any trimmings they can give you when you buy your tree.

Top these up with evergreens or other greenery from the garden. Stick a few robins in, or clusters of baubles.

Make sure that anything placed round the fireplace is very securely fixed, and preferably not inflammable if you have an open fire, because of health and safety.

PACKING UP

Decorations need to be wrapped up and stored carefully each year. Fragile baubles should be wrapped carefully in tissue paper, bubble wrap, or even kitchen roll, so that they are completely covered. If your decorations came in boxes, use these; otherwise, shoe boxes work well, or plastic boxes with lids (I bought some recently for this purpose and am very happy about it). Take care not to overfill the boxes, and mark them 'FRAGILE' in case you (or someone else) forget what is inside. Taking the decorations down can feel like a bit of an anti-climax, but packing them up nicely will make your life so much easier come the following Christmas – and before you know it, it will be that time again!

Wreaths: It's nice to make or buy a wreath for your front door as something to welcome people. Just remember that you need to buy lights suitable for outdoor use.

APPENDIX

There is no definitive guide to how often you should carry out household tasks. How often you need to clean the oven will really depend on how much you use it. What's more, there are always going to be days or weeks when something has to give . . . and don't I know it. However, much like my nocturnal list-making, I find what is outlined below to be a helpful reminder of what might be done, and roughly when.

DAILY

- Air and make the bed.

- Wipe down kitchen counters, kitchen sink and tap.

- Wipe down hobs, Aga surfaces and plates.

- Sweep the kitchen floor.

- Run dishcloths, washing-up brushes and sponges through the dishwasher.

- Run and empty the dishwasher / wash and dry by hand.

- Plump sofa and armchair pillows.

ONCE (OR MORE OFTEN) A WEEK

- Change bed linen.

- Wash tea towels.

- Wash hand towels, bath towels and bath mats.

- Vacuum carpets and rugs.

- Vacuum upholstered furniture, curtains and blinds with the upholstery brush attachment; use the soft brush for vacuuming the tops of books on shelves and light fixtures.

- Rotate sofa and armchair cushions.

- Sweep and mop hard-surfaced floors.

- Dust surfaces.

- Clean mirrors.

- Clean the loo, bathroom sink, shower and bath.

- Empty and clean the fridge and throw out anything past its best.

- Clean microwave.

- Clean the filter in the tumble dryer.

- Rinse out bins after refuse collection day.

- Sort through mail, paperwork, newspapers and magazines, throw out anything that is no longer needed, and reply to anything that needs replying to.

- Water houseplants and window boxes.

- Change flower water.

- Take out the rubbish, recycling and food waste.

- Test smoke and carbon monoxide alarms.

MONTHLY

- Clean dishwasher (see page 60).

- Wipe down the inside of the oven.

- Clean the insides of windows.

- Clean the filters in the washing machine and dishwasher.

- Wash shower curtains.

EVERY 3–6 MONTHS

- Defrost freezer and make an inventory of what's inside.

- Remove items from kitchen cupboards and shelves and clean them.

- Deep clean the oven.

- Sort through medicine cupboard and throw out anything out of date.

- Vacuum and turn mattresses.

- Wash duvets and pillows.

- Beat rugs outside and leave to air.

- Clean washing machine detergent drawer and filter; run an empty cycle to clean the drum.

- Have windows professionally cleaned, if necessary.

- Polish wooden furniture.

- Vacuum under and behind furniture.

YEARLY

———

- Deep clean carpets.

- Polish wooden floors.

- Re-sand and oil wooden worktops or chopping boards.

- Have chimney swept, a month or so before you want to use the fire.

- Service your boiler before winter sets in.

- Service your Aga, if required.

- Replace smoke alarm and carbon monoxide alarm batteries.

- Clean out wardrobe and mothproof woollens. Spring clean and sort out items to give away.

USEFUL WEBSITES

Royal Horticultural Society (RHS)
For expert information on gardening and flowers and details
on membership and events. Mary is an RHS Ambassador. rhs.org.uk

National Garden Scheme (NGS)
Mary is President of the NGS, which opens gardens for charity.

Which.co.uk
For unbiased advice on brands and appliances.

NOTES

KITCHEN KNOW-HOW

CLEANING *&* CONFIGURING YOUR HOME

LAUNDRY & WARDROBE WISDOM

GARDENING & FLOWERS

HOSTING & ADDING THE EXTRA TOUCHES

NOTES

NOTES

NOTES

ACKNOWLEDGEMENTS

The idea for this book came from the lovely Louise Moore, boss of Michael Joseph at Penguin, whom we adore. It took a little while for the concept to sink in, as it's not a cookery book, but with Lucy Young's modern practical ideas and my experience over a lifetime, we were raring to go. Lucy has been by my side for 27 years and we are a team.

A big thank you to Sophie Missing, who interpreted our scribbled notes and put them into a logical order. She has an enquiring mind and being newly married was so keen to learn about our tips and tricks and put them into practice; it was a pleasure to share them with her.

The great team at Michael Joseph, led by Fiona Crosby, have produced a beautiful book. Thank you to John Hamilton, Lee Motley, Sarah Fraser, Alison O'Toole, Gail Jones, Alice Chandler, Aimie Price, Emma Brown and Annie Lee. The photo shoots were masterminded by wonderful Georgia Glynn Smith, always fun to work with, and the results are stunning. Thank you also to Emma Lahaye, props stylist.

Publicist Clare Parker is a one-off, and a joy to have fun with on the book tour, thank you.

Thank you to them all.

Mary

INDEX

PICTURE CREDITS

The publisher is grateful for permission to reproduce the images on the following pages:

Front cover photography copyright © Georgia Glynn Smith, as well as pages 2, 9, 16, 19, 30, 59, 65, 90, 94, 95, 96, 97, 100, 105, 107, 133, 145, 150, 163, 168, 173, 179, 184, 187, 191, 196–7, 219, 222, 223, 227, 229, 236, 239, 240, 242, 250, 255, 256, 261, 262, 265 and 273.

Additional photography as follows:

Page 224 copyright © Camera Press, London.

Pages 205, 211, 212, 216, 217, 224, 225 and 235 copyright © Gap Gardens.

Pages 9, 27, 36, 48, 53, 56, 66, 73, 103, 111, 112, 139, 141, 142, 148 and 232 copyright © Gap Interiors.

Pages 54 and 261 copyright © Gallery Stock.

Pages 198, 202–203, 205, 206, 209, 213, 215 and 216 copyright © BBC Gardener's World Magazine/Jason Ingram.

Pages 9, 37, 40–41, 50, 86, 119, 134, 157, 160, 166, 174, 180, 183, 189 and 224 copyright © Getty Images.

Pages 4–5, 9, 26, 32, 34, 44, 74, 82, 95, 108, 121, 125, 148, 149, 154, 172, 183, 234, 241, 267 and 271 copyright © Loupe.

Page 9, 39, 45, 61, 67, 70, 78, 79, 92, 105, 115, 116, 124, 127, 130, 131, 138, 147, 155, 156, 161, 165, 177, 180, 192, 220, 221, 223, 230, 258, 262, 268 and 270 copyright © Narratives.

Pages 7, 10, 42, 47, 84 and 85 copyright © Nicky Adams.

Pages 63, 88, 159 and back cover copyright © Plainpicture.

Page 247 copyright © Stockfood.

MICHAEL JOSEPH

UK | USA | Canada | Ireland | Australia
India | New Zealand | South Africa

Michael Joseph is part of the Penguin Random House group of companies
whose addresses can be found at global.penguinrandomhouse.com.

First published 2017
001

Text copyright © Mary Berry and Lucy Young, 2017
Illustrations copyright © Ryn Frank, 2017

The moral right of the copyright holders has been asserted

Colour reproduction by Altaimage Ltd
Printed and bound by Firmengruppe APPL, Germany

A CIP catalogue record for this book is available from the British Library

ISBN: 978-0-718-18544-2

www.greenpenguin.co.uk

ABOUT THE AUTHORS

MARY BERRY is the nation's favourite baker and author of over seventy books. She was the much-loved judge on BBC TV show *The Great British Bake Off* and has been teaching the nation to cook, on TV and in her books, for over four decades. Cordon Bleu trained in Paris, Mary began her career as a magazine cookery editor before publishing her first cookery book in 1966. In 2009 Mary was awarded the highly coveted Guild of Food Writers Lifetime Achievement Award and in 2012 she was made a CBE in the Queen's Birthday Honours list.

LUCY YOUNG has worked as a cookery writer and assistant to Mary for nearly thirty years. She is Cordon Bleu trained, with an expertise in Aga cooking, and has authored eight books.

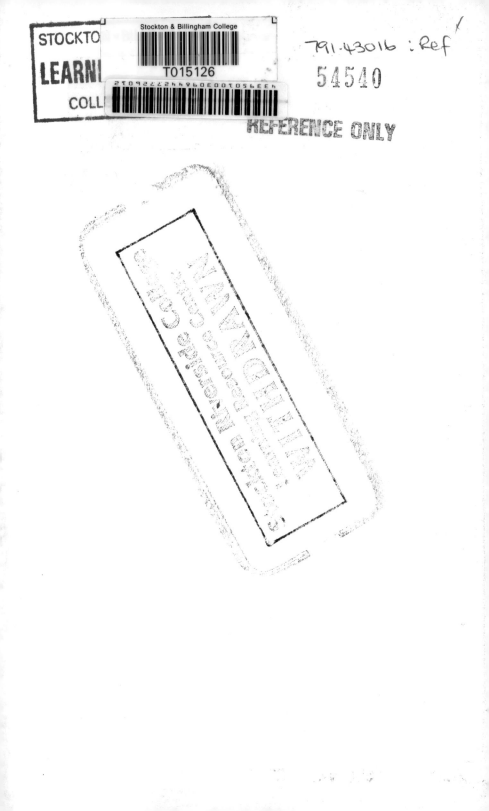